Special Trees
& Woods
of the
Chilterns

First published in Great Britain in 2010 by
Chiltern Woodlands Project Ltd
The Lodge, 90 Station Road, Chinnor
Oxon OX39 4HA

Registered charity no. 1002512
Registered in England as company no. 2357329

ISBN: 978-0-95357-732-3

0953577325

www.chilternsaonb.org/special

Compiled and edited by Rachel Sanderson

Cover design, text design and typesetting by Marie Hanson

Printed and bound in Spain by Graficas Cems

Special Trees & Woods *of the* Chilterns

DESIGNED BY
MARIE HANSON

EDITED BY
RACHEL SANDERSON

Contents

Acknowledgements... 8

Foreword... 10

Introduction... 12

BEDFORDSHIRE

Sharpenhoe Clappers... 20

Witches Beech... 22

Whipsnade Tree Cathedral... 24

BERKSHIRE

Murderous Marker... 30

Clayfield Copse... 32

George's Cedar... 34

BUCKINGHAMSHIRE

Burnham Beeches... 38

Blasted Oak... 44

Bulstrode Camp... 46

Ibstone Yew... 50

Low Scrubs... 52

Turville Park Lime Avenue... 54

Elephant Tree... 56

Giant Cherry... 58

Mushroom Tree... 60

Naphill Common... 62

Umbrella Tree... 66

The Shoe Tree... 68

Palace Plane... 70

Parsonage Wood... 72

Priestfield Arboretum... 76

Crucifix Tree... 80

Tylers Green Memorial Trees... 82

Cliveden... 86

Taplow Tulip... 90

The 'Greatest Ash'... 92

Remnantz Walnut... 94

Sparky's Ash... 96

BUCKINGHAMSHIRE CONT...

Pullingshill Wood... 98

Pulpit Hill... 100

Penn Wood... 102

Hodgemoor Wood... 106

Queen Elizabeth Oak... 110

Fawley Court... 112

Bottom Wood... 114

HERTFORDSHIRE

Woods of the Whippendell Valley... 118

Ashridge... 124

War Wounds... 130

Hockeridge and Pancake Woods... 132

Abbey Pagoda... 134

Domesday Oak... 136

Croxley Green's Commemorative Trees... 138

OXFORDSHIRE

Fair Mile...   142

Jimmy's Tree...   144

Hunts Green Cedar...   146

The Maharajah's Well and Cherry Orchard...   147

Memorial Avenue...   148

Scots Farm Oaks...   150

Nettlebed Woods...   152

Victoria Cross...   154

APENDICES

The Why and How of Tree Measurement...   158

History of the Chiltern Bodgers...   164

Glossary of Terms and Useful Links...   166

Trees Mentioned in the Text: Scientific Names...   168

Contributors...   170

An old oak in the Gade valley, Hertfordshire

Acknowledgements

The publication of this book was made possible by funding from the Chilterns Conservation Board's Sustainable Development Fund.

We are grateful to the Heritage Lottery Fund for their financial support from 2006 to 2010 which made the Special Trees and Woods Project possible.

The Chilterns Conservation Board also provided financial support, office accommodation and use of a section of their website for the Chilterns AONB.

We are indebted to the two members of staff who coordinated the work of the Project, first Liz Manley and then Rachel Sanderson, and who made it such a success.

The book could not have happened without the volunteers, the steering group and everyone else who shared their stories of trees and woods with us.

Finally, we would like to pay special tribute to Marie Hanson whose individual contribution in time, care and design expertise helped to ensure the completion of the book.

In search of Bluebells by Margaret Taperell

Foreword

Remarkable trees are a part of our lives. Many of us remember fondly the elms which were landmarks in our countryside. I travelled the length and breadth of Britain and Ireland to research my first book on trees. I chose 60 individual trees or tree groups striking for their age, size, form or special association such as history or legend. Two of them are an oak and a beech, old friends on my land at Tullynally in Westmeath, Ireland.

Given the same task, someone else would have chosen other trees. This book is a tribute to trees in five counties of southern England chosen by those who know and love them. The Ibstone Yew is a massive churchyard tree in a remote corner of the Chiltern Hills where red kites float across the sky. The Frithsden Beeches are within the National Trust property of Ashridge. Their age and shape excite our imagination and appear in films such as a recent version of *Robin Hood*. Parsonage Wood echoes the grisly story of the 16th century Amersham Martyrs. Sharpenhoe Clappers was a medieval rabbit warren with Iron Age and Roman links jutting out over the Bedford plain. The Fair Mile was planted with elm trees in the 1750s and was much admired in the Henley area. The trees were felled 180 years later and replaced with turkey oaks to mark the coronation of Her Majesty Queen Elizabeth II. In 1978, a further avenue of lime trees was planted to mark the Queen's Silver Jubilee.

Thanks are due to the Heritage Lottery for seeing the value of this Special Trees and Woods Project and for providing supporting funds. Guidance has come from the Chiltern Woodlands Project and the Chilterns Conservation Board. The prime credit goes to the project volunteers who have done the research and recording.

This is their book.

Thomas Pakenham

Introduction

This book is a celebration of the trees and woods of the Chilterns. More than that it is a celebration of the people of the Chilterns and the stories and social history connected to the trees and woods. It is the work of a hundred volunteers who worked from 2006 to 2010 on a Heritage Lottery Funded project coordinated by Liz Manley and then Rachel Sanderson, who worked for the Chiltern Woodlands Project.

The Chilterns are a ridge of chalk hills to the north-west of London. The area is just north of the River Thames and stretches from Wallingford and Reading across to Beaconsfield, St Albans, Hitchin and Luton. The chalk ends in a steep scarp slope looking over the Vale of Aylesbury and dips back towards London. This dip slope is dissected by valleys and the hill tops are capped with clay with flints, where most of the woods are found.

THE CHILTERNS NATURAL AREA

*Please see back cover flap for a map showing the location of each story.

The area covered in this book is that of the Chilterns Landscape Character Area which includes all of the Chilterns Area of Outstanding Natural Beauty (AONB) and the adjoining towns and villages. We must also thank the Chilterns Conservation Board for their support, both financial and in kind through the provision of space in their offices and also on the Chilterns AONB website. Please see *www.chilternsaonb. org/special* for an interactive map with many more stories and other information about this project.

The Chilterns are one of the most heavily wooded regions of England. The area is famous for its ancient beechwoods. Most of these woods are found on the tops of the hills growing on clay with flint soils and more local deposits of gravels and occasionally sands. The trees add height to the hills and change in colour and appearance through the seasons. The Chiltern Hills are an ancient landscape, characterised by relatively small arable and pasture fields, commons, ancient trackways and of course the woods.

An ancient wood is one that has remained continuously wooded since 1600 AD. Many woods are much older, but the trees, unless they were coppiced which often prolongs their lives, are likely to be considerably younger than this. These woods have had a very long history of management. We are finding evidence of Iron Age and Roman iron smelting in some woods. Later in the medieval period it was an important fuel supply for London; with ports on the river Thames such

as Henley and Marlow developing into Riverside towns to send firewood down river on barges to the capital. This is likely to be when many of the wood banks were created.

As mentioned before, 100 volunteers have helped us to record the fascinating stories behind over 770 trees and 168 woods, spread right across the Chilterns. These volunteers received training at 39 weekend events organised by first Liz and then Rachel, who between them developed and coordinated the work programme.

More recently the woods have been the work place of the bodgers who turned chair parts on pole lathes to be assembled in furniture factories around High Wycombe and other wood-wares in Chesham (see page 162 for more information). The famous Windsor chairs were made in the Chilterns for over 200 years and sent down the Thames from Windsor to London and then around the world. Sine the Second World War these furniture industries using local timber have declined. They locally grown beech has been replaced by both imported timber and alternative, but less sustainable, materials such as plastic and metal.

The aims of the Special Trees and Woods Project were to record special trees and woods, gather supporting information, promote the special trees and woods, celebrate the heritage of Chiltern woods and to achieve all this with the involvement of the local community.

Two highlights of this work programme were an art exhibition in 2007 and an art competition the following year. The latter attracted over 150 entries inspired by 79 different Chiltern woods. Images of some of the pieces of art are published in this book. The image below was the winner of the public vote (see foreword for the judges favourite).

Winter Beech by Rachel Wallace

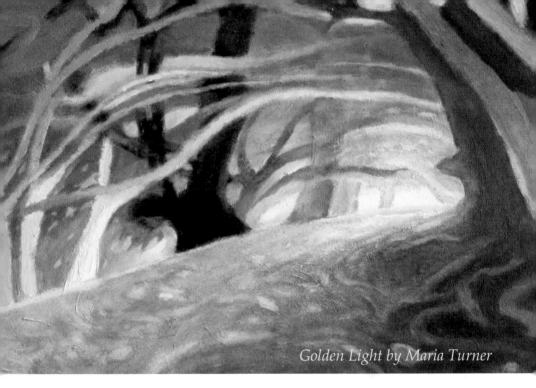

Golden Light by Maria Turner

So what makes a tree special? There is no firm definition as we each find trees special for different reasons. For some, special trees were planted as a celebration, others have a distinctive shape, are of historical interest, are a local landmark, are old and big or simply have an interesting story to tell!

The Chilterns' rich heritage of trees includes some surprising stories which are in danger of being forgotten. This book aims to share some of the best.

Unfortunately the trees and woods of the Chilterns are at risk due to changing climate, which may alter where particular tree species can grow. Other trees are threatened by an increasing range of pests and diseases, from fungi and bacteria, through insect attack to damage by mammals such as browsing of young saplings by deer and bark stripping by grey squirrels. The woods are at risk of neglect and or damage by insensitive use of heavy forestry machinery. There is also increasing concerns about 'Health and Safety' which make old roadside trees particularly vulnerable to either surgery or removal. We hope this project and this book will provide a record in a changing world.

Historically trees were managed in a variety of ways, but now many of the woods are 'high forest' with large tall trees of mainly beech, giving a cathedral-like appearance and the shade leaving a bare ground floor. In the distant past many woods were coppiced, using simple handtools, and the shoots from the cut stool allowed to re-grow to provide a succession of poles and firewood. Other woods were managed as wood pasture, where livestock could graze beneath the trees and pigs could feed on beech mast and acorns in autumn. In these areas trees may have been pollarded, ie cut out of reach of grazing animals. More recently plantations of introduced species, including many conifers, have changed the landscape and added evegreen trees to the mosaic of habitats.

Some of the trees in this book are old, others are large, some are curiosities, some have associations with interesting or important people and a few trees commemorate people. We have decided to include the stories that link our 'special' trees and woods to wider community interests.

We hope this book will inspire you to visit the Chilterns throughout the year, to enjoy the changing seasons from the bare trees of winter, through the bluebell woods of spring, to the cool shade of a beechwood in summer and then the rich colours of autumn.

John Morris
Project Director - September 2010

The large tree known as Waller's Oak at Coleshill has now gone. The photo courtesy of Amersham Museum, was taken in 1887. It is said that the poet and politician Edmund Waller (1605-1687) composed some of his verses on a bench built into this hollow tree, some two hundred years before this photo was taken.

WALLER'S OAK
COLESHILL

C. WARD

Bedfordshire

SHARPENHOE CLAPPERS

WITCHES BEECH

WHIPSNADE TREE CATHEDRAL

Sharpenhoe Clappers

Sharpenhoe Clappers occupies a steep spur on the northern Chilterns escarpment in southern Bedfordshire. It comprises the earthwork remains of two terraces on the northern slope and two banks which run across the spur to the south. It was believed to be an Iron Age promontory fort, but a small archaeological excavation carried out in 1979 suggested that the site has a more complicated history.

The excavation showed that the banks were in fact of medieval date and had been built as a rabbit warren. The existence of warrens in the Sharpenhoe area is suggested by the name 'Clappers', which derives from the French for rabbit warren or 'land with rabbit burrows'. Rabbit warrens provided a consistent supply of meat and skins and were a large part of the economy of the time.

Despite this later than expected date, the investigations found that it was overlying earlier features, including a ditch and a palisade trench which would once have held timber posts. These features date to the Iron Age and artefacts from both this and the Roman period have also been found at the site. The geography of the area certainly makes it a suitable location for a promontory fort. The natural steep slopes to the north, west and east would have been easy to defend, whilst anyone approaching from the south would have been seen well before they arrived.

A beech wood has covered the plateau that might have been the interior of the hill fort since the middle of the 19th century and the woodland and monument are owned and managed by the National Trust. It was donated to the National Trust by W A Robertson in memory of his brothers, Captain Norman Cairns Robertson who died on 20th June 1917 and Lieutenant Laurence Grant Robinson, killed at the Battle of the Somme on 30th July 1916. It is recognised as a nationally important site and is protected as a Scheduled Ancient Monument.

The beech trees have a remarkable amount of wood carving on them, some the result of repeat visits over a number of years which demonstrates the strong personal attachments people have to these trees.

Signposted National Trust car park off minor road halfway between Sharpenhoe and Streatley. Approach also via A6 roundabout signed Streatley. **Grid: TL066296**

Witches Beech

This ancient beech has a massive girth of 6.39m, its size and striking appearance making it a well known landmark of Whipsnade Heath. Its name suggests that this distinctive tree may have a place in local legend.

The Witches Beech may have had some connection to the infamous Dunstable Witch, Elizabeth Pratt, who lived nearby. Elizabeth was accused of bewitching the landlord of the Nags Head's two children, touching both on the head after visiting the pub for bread and ale. After her visit, the children grew sick, with a strange distemper, and died, screaming that they had been murdered by the witch.

Elizabeth was tried as a witch and burned at the stake. Her fate is now remembered in a poem called *The Bottled Curse* by Alfred Wire. At her death, she is said to have cursed the churchyard, leading the local people to avoid it lest her magic attack them, causing the church to fall into disrepair:

> *'Thus the churchyard goes to ruin*
> *Graves and fences getting worse:*
> *Everyone devoutly wishing*
> *Not to free the bottled curse.'*

This tree is on Whipsnade Heath which is owned by the National Trust. Whipsnade Heath is open access land and the tree can be seen from the permissive path around the wood. The Nags Head was near the common at Whipsnade but is now a private house.

Park in Whipsnade Heath car park, at the junction of B4540 and B4541. Walk to the seat in the central glade, turn left and follow the circular path. At northern corner, turn left and follow the path to the tree. **Grid: TL016180**

Whipsnade Tree Cathedral

There is a cathedral-like quality to many of the beech woods in the Chilterns, but a quiet corner of Whipsnade is the site of a Tree Cathedral with a very special story.

The Tree Cathedral was planted during the depression of the 1930s by Edmund Kell Blyth, a member of the generation which fought in both World Wars, keeping faith with his friends and comrades who had fallen in the First. The Cathedral bears witness to the ideals which had sustained them – a love of nature, a spirit of service and a belief that the two are linked. These same ideals animated the founders of the National Trust and the Tree Cathedral, bringing this important connection into focus.

The Chancel is a semi-circle of silver birch in front of a yew hedge

But the Tree Cathedral is not a war memorial. EK Blyth had been looking for a project that would express a sense of purpose and meaning of life in memory of his friends. His moment of inspiration came in 1930 after visiting the new Liverpool Anglican Cathedral which was then being built, and appreciating what a wonderful and inspiring project it must be for those involved. Clearly, to build a real cathedral would be beyond his means. On his journey home to the Chilterns he saw a stand of trees lit by the evening sun. It occurred to him then that here was something even more beautiful, and that one could form a cathedral with trees.

'The Christmas Chapel looks at its best in the winter months'

It is formed by trees that are planted in the shape of a traditional medieval cathedral and is managed to emphasise the vigour and balance of individual plants, in patterns that create interconnected enclosures. These beautiful spaces in the Tree Cathedral encourage contemplation and spiritual thought.

The plan follows closely that of a great cathedral with a nave and transepts, a Lady Chapel and an outer Cloister Walk enclosing a wide area with a 'Dew Pond' enclosure as its central point. Because it is not consecrated as a Church, there is no formal altar or cross; instead the Chancel is a semi-circle of silver birches. Its serene beauty makes it popular as a venue for wedding blessings.

There are four chapels of the seasons with appropriate trees: Easter, cherries in blossom; Christmas, Norway spruce; summer, whitebeam and rowan red berries; and autumn, colours provided by beech and field maple.

Every visit to the Tree Cathedral is different as the trees respond to changes in the weather and seasons, and as they mature and are gradually replaced. This constant state of development adds to the Tree Cathedral's interest, shifting the emphasis of its management away from 'conservation' (as would be the case for a historical monument) towards a more interactive process which needs to take account of its dynamic nature.

The Tree Cathedral is open every day of the year and entrance is free.

'The Nave is defined by a beautiful avenue of lime trees'

Signposted from B4540, Whipsnade Village. Two miles south of Dunstable.
For more information contact the Trustees of the Whipsnade Tree Cathedral Fund on 01582
872406 or visit www.nationaltrust.org.uk **Grid: TL008181**

Berkshire

MURDEROUS MARKER

CLAYFIELD COPSE

GEORGE'S CEDAR

n 1441 A Nun &

A Monk here slain

"for 'm' conduct'

and byried under

he Yew Tree.

Murderous Marker

Located in the garden of The Bull at Streatley, this yew tree marks the spot of a reputedly grizzly crime...

> *'In 1440 a nun and*
> *a monk here slain*
> *for misconduct*
> *and buried under*
> *the yew tree'*

Sadly we have no way of authenticating the story.

This tree grows by the path between the car park and the back door of The Bull pub at Streatley (A417). **Grid: SU591807**

Clayfield Copse

Clayfield Copse is on the edge of Caversham Park, first mentioned in records dating from 1223 when King Henry III gave ten deer to the owner, the Earl of Pembroke. The old boundary of Caversham Park runs as a curving bank through Clayfield Copse.

There is a long history of mineral extraction in this complex of woods. The old clay pit in Blackhouse Wood was dug to make bricks at the nearby works in Kiln Road from 1645 and old chalk mines lie beneath the trees we see today.

Large car park off Caversham Park Village Road. Pedestrian entrances in Kiln Road (Emmer Green to Binfield Heath road) and Foxhill Lane. **Grid: SU725772**

The wood has a number of wild service trees and there is an even rarer wild pear tree in the hedgerow on the edge of the old lane by Blackhouse Wood. The presence of these species is a good indication that the wood is ancient woodland as they are rarely planted.

Clayfield Copse was part of the first Local Nature Reserve designated by Reading Borough Council in 1991.

CLAYFIELD DRAGON

Clayfield Copse has a ferocious neighbour; a dragon lying in guard at its edge!

An old oak was heavily pollarded in 2006, producing several very large pieces of wood, and the Emmer Green Residents' Association decided it was a great opportunity for some community art. In consultation with local children, a dragon was picked as the sculpture of choice. It was then designed and carved by local wood turner Andrew Noyes. The dragon has since become a local attraction, and provides a great backdrop for art displays and story-telling events within the community.

George's Cedar

There are many large cedars in the grounds of Park Place but only one of them can claim to have such an unusual and distinguished history; it was planted by King George III when he was a child.

From 1738 until his death in 1751, George III's father Frederick Prince of Wales owned Park Place where the tree stands. George was born in the same year the house was purchased. Due to a quarrel between the King (George II) and the Prince of Wales (George III's father), the family spent most of their time in the country. This tree is thought to have been planted by George III sometime before his 14th birthday.

George's cedar, on the back lawn of Park Place, and the others found in the grounds, have been a definitive part of the landscape around the house for centuries; George's cedar is visible to the right of the house in an aerial photo from 1949 (below). The tree still stands in the grounds of Park Place and is perhaps a more dignified legacy to an old king than the madness that marred the end of his reign, for which he is usually remembered.

For many years Park Place was a boarding school and former teachers and pupils have fond memories of the grounds. The school closed in 1988 and Park Place is now in private ownership.

In grounds of Park Place. This is now a private residence. **Grid: SU777822**

Buckinghamshire

BURNHAM BEECHES

BLASTED OAK

BULSTRODE CAMP

IBSTONE YEW

LOW SCRUBS

TURVILLE PARK LIME AVENUE

ELEPHANT TREE

GIANT CHERRY

MUSHROOM TREE

NAPHILL COMMON

UMBRELLA TREE

THE SHOE TREE

PALACE PLANE

PARSONAGE WOOD

PRIESTFIELD ARBORETUM

CRUCIFIX TREE   PULLINGSHILL WOOD

TYLERS GREEN   PULPIT HILL

CLIVEDEN   PENN WOOD

TAPLOW TULIP   HODGEMOOR WOOD

GREATEST ASH   QUEEN ELIZABETH OAK

REMNANTZ WALNUT   FAWLEY COURT

SPARKY'S ASH   BOTTOM WOOD

Burnham Beeches

Burnham Beeches has a long history of woodland management and habitation. There are three Scheduled Ancient Monuments in the woods which show the area was home to people as early as the Iron Age. The woods were, for centuries, managed as wood-pasture with livestock grazing beneath the trees which were regularly pollarded. The Domesday Book records Burnham Parish as having 'woodland enough to feed 600 swine'.

This historic landscape was almost lost in 1879 when it was put up for sale as 'land suitable for the erection of superior residences'. Fortunately, one year later it was bought by the City of London. This has preserved it as an open space for the public to explore and enjoy. The Beeches now attracts roughly 500,000 visitors every year and is busiest in the autumn when many come to see the magnificent autumn colours.

Burnham Beeches is a site of international importance for wildlife. As well as the woodland, other habitats include heath, valley mires, coppice, ponds, streams and grassland. This mosaic of habitats creates the best conditions for birds, bats, fungi and other wood-living organisms. Livestock have been re-introduced and visitors may see pigs, sheep, cows and ponies grazing.

Sunlit Beechwoods by Laraine Healey

'After a lengthy walk I sometimes sit beside the lake and recall the memories of what these woods hold, both for me and for past generations. I will always be inspired by the changing beauty of Burnham Beeches.'

Laraine Healey

The Cage Pollard (above) was named so the tree could be included in the 50 Great British Trees recognised to celebrate the Queen's Golden Jubilee. This tree is famous after appearing in the 1991 blockbuster *Robin Hood: Prince of Thieves*, starring Kevin Costner.

Druid's Oak is still standing, though it now has a smaller canopy than shown in this old postcard (left) where it is called 'The Old Druid'. While its canopy may change, its girth of 9m remains huge.

Another of the ancient pollarded beeches

Many of the trees at Burnham Beeches have names as they have formed curious shapes over the years (such as the Ballerina Tree, opposite) and are easily recognisable, not least due to their size.

His Majesty was a giant beech pollard, the oldest and largest in the British Isles. When it fell during the great storm in October 1987, it was estimated to be about 600 years old. In 1989 a replacement tree was planted by the Lord Mayor of London to commemorate the 800th year of the mayoralty of the City of London.

~

Mendelssohn's Tree doesn't rival its remarkable neighbours, with a girth of only 0.12m and a less than impressive height of 3.8m, but it has a special story. This young beech tree was planted to replace the original Mendelssohn's Tree and to commemorate 125 years of ownership of Burnham Beeches by the Corporation of London. It was planted by the Ambassador of the Federal Republic of Germany on 20th October 2005.

The original tree which was a beech pollard suffered storm damage in 1990 and eventually died. It was under this tree that German composer Felix Mendelssohn is said to have found inspiration for some of his music during a visit to England in 1838. A piece of the original tree can be found in the Barbican Centre in London.

~

A plaque in Burnham Beeches (below) marks the site of the original Jenny Lind Tree. Born in Stockholm, this famous soprano (1820–1887) was known all over the world as the 'Swedish Nightingale'. It is said that she would often sit beneath the ancient and gnarled beech studying, memorising and singing her next opera. Long after the demise of the original tree, a young beech was planted in 1987 to mark the centenary of her death by the Swedish Ambassador, Mr Leif Leifland. 20 years later, this new beech is thriving, already reaching a height of 14m.

Main access to Burnham Beeches is from the A355 Slough-Beaconsfield road at Farnham Common. Full details are available on the City of London website.
Grid: SU958850

'After various attempts to lift the large piece of wreckage there was a mighty crack as the tree trunk split'

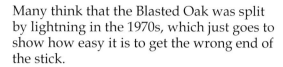

Blasted Oak

Many think that the Blasted Oak was split by lightning in the 1970s, which just goes to show how easy it is to get the wrong end of the stick.

Michael Dady now lives in Australia, but he was born in Chivery and remembers well how the tree split in two. His story begins on a foggy Friday morning, 30th October 1942, when Michael's father, Alf, and his workmates heard a plane crash. They ran more than a mile to the crash site where what is thought to be a Wellington, piloted by and carrying members of the Women's Auxiliary Air Force, had come down near Baldwin's Wood. Michael's father and workmates received commendations for their bravery and resourcefulness at the crash scene. However, despite the best efforts of the local villagers, there were no survivors.

Some days later, Michael was walking with his parents when they saw a party attempting to lift a piece of wreckage with a tractor, to allow an RAF trailer to back underneath it. They had a rope over the sturdy roadside oak but the tractor was struggling. Alf went to help with the clear-up operation while Michael and his mother watched.

After various attempts to lift the large piece of wreckage there was a mighty crack as the tree trunk split.

The sizable split in the massive oak trunk has jeopardised the long term future of this roadside tree, so a brace has been added to offer support and prevent further splitting.

The tree is in a hedge along Taylor's Lane, Chivery, near Wendover.

From Wendover, take Hale Road (just off B4009 to Tring). Turn left into Hale Lane. After approx two miles, pass Hale and Milesfield Farms on left. At the next road junction the tree will be straight ahead. **Grid: SP902073**

Bulstrode Camp

Tucked away near the centre of Gerrards Cross village are some of the oldest oak trees in the Chilterns. These majestic oaks grow on Bulstrode Camp, an Iron Age hill fort dating back to around 400 BC.

Bulstrode Camp is a flat open area covering just over nine hectares and surrounded by a double ring of ramparts, still impressive despite being eroded and overgrown in places. When writing about Bulstrode Park in 1847 in his History and Antiquities of the County of Buckingham Vol VIII, George Lipscomb wrote:

> *'On a hill south-east of the House there is a very large circular entrenchment with some large old oaks growing on its banks.'*

Around 40 of the oaks which seemed old in 1847 still stand today and can now truly be described as ancient. Most are, inevitably, in various stages of decline. Some have already died leaving only dramatically bare skeletons to tell of their former glory; however several others are remarkably healthy, sending out promising new growth each spring.

Many of these ancient oaks date back at least to the late 17th century when the Bulstrode estate was laid out and some are probably older than that. The largest tree of the group has an impressive girth of more than 6m.

These trees have been a well-loved local landmark for many years. Clearly many of them were showing signs of collapse and hollowing around 1900 when dated brickwork was inserted to support them. In some cases the trees have grown over and round these brick in-fills and in others the brickwork has fallen out, but the trees have survived regardless, showing their true resilience. After a period of neglect, the local Parish Council which is now responsible for Bulstrode Camp and these very special trees, has written a new management plan, so the trees will survive for decades to come.

There are more huge old trees in Bulstrode Park and along Camp Road which runs around the perimeter of the Camp.

To the west of the B416 Gerrards Cross-Slough road and near the junction with the A40 in Gerrards Cross. Turn into Camp Road – there is a footpath almost opposite the end of the short spur into Camp Road. **Grid: SU995880**

'Some of the oaks have already died leaving only dramatically bare skeletons to tell of their former glory'

Ibstone Yew

As you can see from the photo, this tree is enormous. Its girth is a whopping 5.6m, making it one of the largest yews found in the Chilterns by the Special Trees and Woods Project. The tree is also very tall, dwarfing the medieval parish church of St Nicholas beside which it grows.

The mainly Norman church dates from before the 12th century and evidence has been found of ancient dwellings around the church in the surrounding area. The church now sits in solitary splendour on a south-facing ridge, deserted by the villagers who moved about a mile to the north and built a new village there. The old village was probably abandoned after the Black Death (bubonic plague) in 1348 which killed about a third of the population; the Yew survived.

Local legend has it that an attempt was made to build a new church in the present village, but the Devil objected to the site and destroyed the structure thereby giving the name of Hell Corner to the spot.

In 1958, Swanton published a book on the Yews of England. He wrote:

> 'The church is in a very secluded spot high up on the hills; Mr Giltrow and I measured it on October 15th, 1954. The trunk is not hollow and there is much spray on it. Girth about 18ft 6ins. The crown of nine branches has an umbrage 61ft in diameter.'

The yew is reputedly over 1,000 years old. The trunk is quite hollow in places and the holes have been filled with concrete. In the past hollow trees were often treated like this in an attempt to preserve them by reducing rot. This practice is now rarely carried out.

This girth measurement equates to roughly 5.6m, so the tree has hardly grown in the last 60 years. The 'spray' referred to was very thick side branches. The wonderfully knobbly trunk we see on this tree now shows that yew trees can look better by removing what is often scrappy growth around the lower trunk.

The tree is in the churchyard at the south end of Ibstone. From the Stokenchurch-Fingest road, turn into Manor Farm Lane. Where the lane turns sharp left, go straight on. The church is signposted. **Grid: SU755923**

Low Scrubs

Contrary to its rather shabby sounding name, Low Scrubs is a striking and mysterious area of woodland.

The wood is an ancient coppice and may be home to some of the oldest beech trees in the Chilterns. The trees were formerly used by the local people as a free source of firewood and grow on land which was previously a wooded common. In 1805 an Inclosure Award vested the land in the hands of Trustees of two charities which represented the 'poor inhabitants of Ellesborough'.

Low Scrubs continued to be a valuable resource for the locals until the end of the Second World War. One resident of the area, Mr Wells, vividly recalled the past use of the woodland when he shared his memories with the Special Trees and Woods Project. Those with rights to collect wood at Low Scrubs each had an area of the wood containing a number of trees that they called their own. Mr Wells said they were allowed to cut as much as they liked, but 'were not allowed to use a saw … just a chopper, an axe … to collect whatever they were able to cut'. People would make 'little stacks of wood in their area and [other] people would never touch it'. The bundles would then be carried or pulled down the hill home to Dunsmore.

Managing trees by coppicing usually involves cutting the tree down to ground level. It then re-grows with multiple stems which can be harvested sustainably at regular intervals. At Low Scrubs, commoners may have lopped off suitable sized branches rather than cut the whole stool down to ground level. The wood was then cut into logs, split into billets, or young branches bundled as faggots. Some might have been burnt on site to make charcoal or potash. The long history of coppicing has caused the trees to grow with the 'witches broom' effect. In some beech trees, this effect is the result of changes in the plant hormones which mean the tree produces clusters of new shoots following wounding made when the tree was regularly cut for firewood.

Trees which have been subject to the same management practices for centuries can become vulnerable when management ceases. The Special Trees and Woods Project used Low Scrubs as a case study site for a workshop at which the management of ancient beech coppice was discussed. Following careful assessment and sensitive pruning, the trees at Low Scrubs are responding well and once again producing new growth. Hopefully this will ensure the trees live on for many more decades to come.

National Trust (Coombe Hill) car park. Take the road linking the A413 and A4010. At Ellesborough crossroads, turn south for approx three quarters of a mile. Turn left, uphill, to car park – approx half a mile. **Grid: SP852062**

Turville Park Lime Avenue

The Turville Park Lime Avenue is in the Manor of Turville Heath, historically held by the Abbey of St Albans until the dissolution of the monasteries in 1539. By 1721 the Manor had been divided into six parts, one of which eventually came into the ownership of William Perry, who was High Sheriff of the county in 1741. Perry rebuilt the house and, as part of his landscaping, planted the Avenue in 1740; the Small-leafed Lime he used is believed to originate from native stock in the Wye Valley. Some of these trees remain today, and are now fine veterans.

The Pinocchio tree (below right) is one of the oldest trees in Lime Avenue. One explanation of its unusual growth is that it originally had just one trunk, which became hollow over time as the inside rotted. The tree then sent out an adventitious root which took hold inside the fertile rotten trunk and began to grow. As the old trunk broke up and healed around the wound, the lesser trunk became more prominent.

Over the years, the house suffered considerably from Victorian additions and 'improvements', which were subsequently demolished by owners in the 20th century. Gaps in Lime Avenue were filled as trees were lost, most notably after a great gale in the 1880s, however these new plantings were hybrid limes of various sub-species.

The years of neglect meant that the Avenue was in a parlous state when Turville Park came into Lord Sainsbury's ownership in 1996. Sainsbury, realising the landscape and historical value of Lime Avenue, voluntarily accepted responsibility for both sides of the road and instigated a programme of management, including regular inspection and careful tree surgery where necessary. He created a stock pool of young trees vegetatively propagated from the original stock which has been used to replace any further veterans lost.

New limes planted as part of his restoration work are now well established, continuing the genotype of the original plantings. Thus, the future of this interesting avenue now, thankfully, appears assured.

The avenue is at Turville Heath, one and a quarter miles south-east of Northend on the lane towards Stonor and Henley-on-Thames. **Grid: SU742913**

Elephant Tree

Regular walkers in Common Wood, near Tylers Green, all know the Elephant Tree as a local landmark.

The Elephant Tree is in fact two trees which have fused together in a remarkable manner. The angles of growth appear to create 'dimples' on the elephant's face and the distinctive grey colouring of the beech adds to the illusion.

Common Wood is owned by the Penn and Tylers Green Residents Society. As its name implies, Common Wood was once an area of common land over which local residents had rights of access for grazing of animals and collecting firewood, etc. In the 19th century the wood passed into private ownership, but continued to be used for recreation by members of the local community. In 2002 it was put up for sale in small lots and, after much fundraising, the Residents Society bought the wood to help preserve it in perpetuity for public enjoyment.

A close-up of the Elephant Tree reveals its distinctive features

At Tylers Green (on the Hazlemere-Beaconsfield road), turn east at the crossroads along Penn Bottom road. Park near the public footpath sign. Walk north uphill for approx 450m and the Elephant Tree is on your left. **Grid: SU910947**

Giant Cherry

This giant cherry tree measures nearly 4m around its girth, a remarkable size which has led the age of the tree to be estimated at around 400 years.

The tree is found in a private garden on Wheeler End Common, which belongs to the Dashwood Estate. It may be a relic of a mixed orchard, as a very old fig and pear tree can be found nearby in an area which was once a farm. It is at its most spectacular each spring when it blossoms with thousands of flowers.

The owner is very proud of his tree and welcomes visitors.

This tree is in a private garden. Visitors are welcome – telephone 01844 355503 to arrange an appointment.
Grid: SU805927

Mushroom Tree

The Mushroom Tree is a hawthorn on the southern edge of Coleshill common that has been shaped for over 60 years.

Albert Bates lived in the flint and brick Thornbury Cottage opposite the tree with his wife, Ada. The couple adopted the Mushroom Tree, and regularly trimmed both the tree and the surrounding grass, which they used as an extension to their garden. On warm summer days they took out chairs and sat beneath the Mushroom Tree to watch the world go by. The grass was also used by Ada as a convenient place to spread her sheets to dry.

Thornbury Cottage was originally two cottages. Local resident Sidney Ware remembers the old lady who lived in one of them sitting at her door and working with her lace pillow and bobbins. The cottages were sold for £75 each and, later, Albert Bates knocked them into one.

After Albert and his wife died the tree was mysteriously tended with an annual cut for several years. When the mystery gardener stopped the Parish Council paid for the tree to be reshaped so that this local landmark was not lost forever. Now an annual trim ensures that Albert's pride and joy is once more a local feature.

*'Mr Albert Bates (85)
beside the mushroom shaped
hawthorn bush opposite his
flint cottage in Chalk Hill'*

*From Amersham Road (between Amersham and Beaconsfield), turn into Coleshill.
The tree is on Coleshill Common at the south end of the village.* **Grid: SU947947**

'On warm summer days they took out chairs and sat beneath the Mushroom Tree to watch the world go by'

Naphill Common

Naphill Common was once a wood-pasture, that is, open grassland dotted with pollarded trees. Cattle and sheep were regularly grazed, which kept the common open. It is thought that in the 18th and early 19th centuries drovers used the common to move cattle from the west towards London.

The enclosure of the parish in the 1860s halved the size of the common, and grazing must have declined because in 1911 local writer G. Eland wrote that:

> *'Among the scattered and misshapen oaks and scrubby beech rise great bushes of juniper and gorse, eight or ten feet high; now all dark with the stalks of dead bracken forming a tangled mass of orange and ochreous lines across them.'*

The grazing finally stopped in the late 1920s. The last farmer to put cows on the common was Arthur Nicholls of Vincent's Farm and they were tended by Ken 'Kedgel' Bristow in 1928. From then on the trees gradually spread, shading out the heathland plants, until the common became mature oak and beech woodland with an understorey of holly. A careful search will reveal remnants of the heathland flora; a patch of heather, some gorse and a few juniper bushes clinging precariously to life.

While open areas survived the common was widely used by villagers. The scouts and guides held meetings there in summer and an annual fair was held on the Broad Path from Victorian times until the 1920s. The parents of Philip and Trevor Hussey first met at the fair on Naphill Common and were married in 1925. A Naphill man himself, when Mr Hussey was asked whether his wife was a local girl he replied 'no, she came from Speen' – a distant village, all of a mile and a half down the road.

This ancient beech stands by a pond on Naphill Common

In the first half of the 20th century the paths of the common provided important routes to High Wycombe, Downley and Bradenham. In the 1930s and 40s Mr and Mrs 'Birdy' Wingrove ran a tiny shop in a meadow beside the common. The Wingroves sold sweets and lemonade to those passing to and from Bradenham and families picnicking by the Umbrella Tree. The cottage is no longer there; all that remains is a small mound in the meadow and pleasant memories.

Veteran Beech by Susan Wharton

Many of the older pollarded oak and beech trees survive today, now surrounded by their offspring. Some are huge and handsome veterans. The Great Beech stands on the bank of what is probably a Romano-British farmstead and overlooks Dew Pond in which a shard of a Romano-British storage jar was found. The so-called Carving Tree (left) has many names and initials carved into the bark, some dating back almost 100 years. A village lad, Albert Smith, who was born in 1897, carved his name there in 1914 before going off to fight in the First World War. He survived to return to Naphill in 1918 and later worked in the local furniture factories. In the Second World War the common was used to test Churchill Tanks and the tracks they gouged out can still be seen under the leaves.

In 1951 Naphill Common was designated a Site of Special Scientific Interest and in 1992 the very rare Starfruit was discovered in one of the many ponds. The common is still popular with walkers and horse riders. In 2008 a new group, The Friends of Naphill Common, was formed to preserve what is special about the common and work to make it more accessible to local people.

To west side of Naphill Village on Hughenden Valley-Lacey Green road. Access via Chapel Lane. Ancient beech and pond at near intersection of footpath H21 and bridleway H2.
Grid: SU840970

Umbrella Tree

A local landmark on the Bradenham side of Naphill Common, the Umbrella Tree has been clipped into its present shape for over 100 years.

A photograph of two girls and a goat with the Umbrella Tree is thought to have been taken between 1890 and 1900. It is thought that the girls are the Tilbury sisters.

The Tilbury sisters appear again, in a postcard, dated 28th August 1906. Their brother Albert (Bert) Tilbury remembered the photograph being taken, and said that they were about to take lunch to their father who worked nearby.

The tree, a hawthorn, was clipped by whoever lived in the nearby cottage. Following the death of the last resident, the tree became neglected for a while until the National Trust, which owns the land on which the tree stands, agreed to tend the tree using the old photographs for guidance.

The tree grows by the bridleway that runs from the Green at Bradenham into Bradenham Woods.

Time and the Umbrella Tree by Trevor Hussey

'The tree has been admired, picnicked under, played round, photographed and sketched. Meanwhile, despite the attention, the tree has inched higher.'

Trevor Hussey

From Bradenham Village (just off the A4010 High Wycombe-Princes Risborough road), follow bridleway along the southern edge of the green. Walk east into Bradenham Woods, following the bridleway to the top of the hill. **Grid: SU832968**

The Shoe Tree

Shoes first appeared in a tree by the A40 near Stokenchurch in the 1970s.

There have been three shoe trees near this spot over recent years. The current tree was 'dressed' by members of the Studley Green youth group who were disappointed when the mature ash tree covered with shoes was vandalised. The vandalism resulted in that tree being felled for safety reasons in 1997. The current shoe tree has recently had its branches cut back, perhaps to stop more shoes being added to it.

There are shoe trees elsewhere in England and throughout the world. Many reasons have been put forward to explain the origins of the practice of hanging shoes in trees. These include fertility rituals, a toll payment by travellers, witchcraft – 'hanging' on your enemies or simply just a local hoax...

Regardless of the reason why people start 'dressing' trees they soon become remarkable landmarks which periodically attract local, national and international interest, not all of which is warranted!

A BBC cameraman taking a close-up of one of the shoes

The tree is on the north side of the A40 West Wycombe-Stokenchurch road and approx a third of a mile west of Studley Green. **Grid: SU782955**

Palace Plane

This inspiring tree has a girth of 8.75m making it the largest London Plane in Buckinghamshire and the Chilterns.

The tree takes its name from the history of the site on which it grows, now the edge of the recreation ground. These playing fields and some of the adjacent residential street Wooburn Manor Park, are on the site of Wooburn Bishops Manor. For nearly 500 years the Manor was owned by the See (or Bishopric or Diocese) of Lincoln. One of the Bishops who held this palace was a member of Henry VIII's Privy Council. The Manor changed hands in 1547 and the palace was pulled down in 1750.

Mr Vinter, who owns the Palace Plane, said:

> 'We have always been very proud of the tree despite its unpractical size in our small garden. It certainly keeps us busy; I collect about 120 sacks of fallen leaves in the autumn!'

As a county champion, the biggest tree of its species in Buckinghamshire, this tree is also listed on the Tree Register of the British Isles.

The Palace Plane towers over its neighbours

This tree is in a private garden but is visible from the public footpath across Wooburn Park to the east of A4094 between Bourne End and Wooburn Green. **Grid: SU913881**

Parsonage Wood

Parsonage Wood (also known as Rectory Wood), on the hill above Old Amersham, appears to be a typical Chiltern beech wood, but it has a sinister past.

In 1521, about 100m from the edge of today's Parsonage Wood, six local men and one woman were burned to death for their religious beliefs. They were Lollards, followers of John Wycliffe of Oxford, who believed that everyone should have the right to read the bible in their own language, not in Latin as prescribed by the Catholic Church. They met secretly, in each other's homes, or perhaps in the local woods where some of them may have worked. The established Church was everywhere engaged in stamping out heresy; many were brutally persecuted around this time.

Close to where the Amersham Martyrs died is a large stone memorial, erected in 1931 by the Protestant Alliance. The sheer horror of their fate is vividly described in Foxe's Book of Martyrs; the brutality is much worse when you learn the gruesome details. Some of the burnings involved the victims' children being forced to light the fire – probably kindled with sticks from nearby Parsonage Wood. Their execution site was well chosen, visible from the town below. The ringleader of the group was allegedly singled out, put in a barrel containing sharpened spikes, and rolled down the hill into the River Misbourne.

William Tillesworth's daughter, Joan Clarke, was compelled to light his pyre and all those ordered to do penance had to carry faggots for the pyre and attend the execution.

THE
NOBLE
ARMY OF
MARTYRS
PRAISE
THEE

AMERSHAM
MARTYRS.

IN THE SHALLOW DEPRESSION AT
A SPOT 100 YARDS LEFT OF THIS
MONUMENT, SEVEN PROTESTANTS, SIX MEN
AND ONE WOMAN WERE BURNED TO DEATH
AT THE STAKE. THEY DIED FOR THE
PRINCIPLES OF RELIGIOUS LIBERTY,
FOR THE RIGHT TO READ AND INTERPRET
THE HOLY SCRIPTURES AND TO WORSHIP
GOD ACCORDING TO THEIR CONSCIENCES
AS REVEALED THROUGH GOD'S HOLY WORD.

THEIR NAMES SHALL LIVE FOR EVER.

WILLIAM TYLSWORTH. BURNED 1506.
(JOAN CLARK, HIS MARRIED DAUGHTER, WAS
COMPELLED TO LIGHT THE FAGGOTS TO BURN HER FATHER.)

THOMAS BARNARD.   BURNED 1521.

JAMES MORDEN.   BURNED 1521.

JOHN SCRIVENER.   BURNED 1521.
(HIS CHILDREN WERE COMPELLED TO LIGHT THEIR FATHER'S PYRE.)

ROBERT RAVE.
                    BURNED 1521.
THOMAS HOLMES.
                    BURNED 1521.
JOAN NORMAN.
                    BURNED 1521.

Local folklore has it that ghosts have been seen and heard in several places; the wood itself and the local Chequers pub, where the condemned folk were held on the eve of their execution. The ringleader is said on occasion to rise out of the River Misbourne near where he drowned.

There are many references to these executions in local literature, but what of Parsonage Wood itself? What is its probable age, how close was it then to the execution site and, in fact, did it even exist as a wood in the 16th century? The wood is clearly shown on early maps (Rocque 1761; Jeffery 1770; Bryant 1825) and its shape seems to have changed little over the centuries; in fact it still has a very pronounced wood bank defining the boundary and almost encircling the wood. In the recent Inventory of Ancient Woodlands it is defined as 'ancient semi-natural woodland' so, on this evidence, it is at least 400 years old.

'This ancient wood has a sinister story'

In Amersham Old Town, follow High Street to west. Turn right by church and follow the narrow lane steeply uphill to wood. Park in Amersham Old Town or Amersham-on-the-Hill. **Grid: SU960978**

Priestfield Arboretum

Priestfield Arboretum, a varied and spectacular collection of conifers and other trees, takes its name from its founder, Thomas Priest.

Thomas Priest began planting trees, particularly conifers, sometime in the 1920s in the orchard and kitchen garden part of the grounds of Harewood Estate soon after the estate was broken up. The arboretum was a labour of love for him and he wished to be buried there when he passed away. After his death the arboretum was sold and it remains in private ownership.

The arboretum fell into disrepair for some years, but in 1983 a massive scrub clearance was carried out by a team of volunteers from The Chiltern Society Small Woodlands Project, the precursor to the Chiltern Woodlands Project. In 1984 the Friends of Priestfield was formed, a group of enthusiastic volunteers who now manage and maintain the site, with the owners' permission. The shelter belts around the site suffered severe damage in the 1987 storm and, when the fallen trees were cleared, an opportunity for new planting arose.

There are now over 200 specimen trees from all over the world to be found at Priestfield. Many of the species are now on the endangered list in their own country. Conifers account for 65% of the collection, representing every genus able to grow in Britain. Amongst the most notable species are the Calva crab apple, the largest of only four trees known in the UK, and a Manchurian fir (above), also extremely rare and the national champion. There are a number of other county champions.

Each year, in June and October, the Friends of Priestfield organise two open days with guided tours.

In Little Kingshill, at the crossroads formed by Heath End Road and Watchet Lane, turn north up the lane lined with houses. On the left, after about 180m, there is a footpath to the arboretum. **Grid: SU900993**

Crucifix Tree

Eric Gill was a sculptor, typographer, and writer who lived at North Dean. The subject matter for his work included both the deeply religious and the highly erotic.

In the 1930s he designed a crucifix which was carved from oak timber by an artistic colleague, Donald Potter. It was nailed to a small beech tree in Pigotts Wood. Gill is said to have taken his daily constitutional to the Crucifix Tree where he said his rosary.

Allegedly, the tree was dying, but after the crucifix was hung it flourished. The tree still survives, though it is not a good specimen of a beech tree.

The original crucifix was removed in 1977 but an oak replica, made by local sculptor Thalia Polak, has been in its place ever since.

There are several footpaths through Pigotts Wood in which this tree grows. The crucifix is hard to spot! Try entering the wood from the north-west corner and take the second path on the right. Keep looking on the right hand side for the tree and don't forget to look up in the branches...

Pigotts Wood is a good place to see bluebells and also has some fine hornbeams on old woodbanks

South-east of Upper North Dean (on the Speen-High Wycombe road), turn north into Piggott's Hill. Drive past Piggotts to the end of the road and park outside the gate to Little Piggotts. **Grid: SU853994**

Tylers Green Memorial Trees

A row of stately lime trees grows on the Back Common in Tylers Green. At the base of two of these eight trees is a small plaque, with a name which also appears on the memorial in St Margaret's Church. The limes are evenly spaced, with two gaps, suggesting that there were originally ten. When and why the trees were planted had been forgotten, so Special Trees and Woods Project volunteers, Russell and Chris Read, decided to research the story.

Handwritten entries in the parish minutes for the immediate post-war years relating to dumping rubbish on the common, the burning of gorse, broken fences, the holding of the annual fair - but there is no mention of the lime trees. Photographs from 1926 also clearly show that the trees were not there then. Could the trees have been planted after the Second World War to commemorate those who had died in both wars?

Further research of the parish minutes for the post-1945 years also drew a blank. An appeal for information in the local parish magazine provided valuable help. Charlie and Doreen Herd, who still live opposite the row of limes came forward with two photographs showing the trees in about 1940 and in1952. In these pictures the saplings look too young to have been planted in 1920 and yet too tall to have been planted after 1945, and so the mystery deepened. Fortunately though William Wheeler, who left the village in 1943, still remembered the trees being planted in the 1930s.

The original photographs provided by Charlie and Doreen Herd

The parish records of January 1937 revealed plans for an avenue of lime trees as part of the Coronation celebrations. For several reasons these plans were not fulfilled and a report of the celebrations on 12th May 1937 in the *Bucks Free Press* contains no mention of the trees. However, in the issue of the 29th October 1937 there was a report of a meeting of the British Legion at which reference was made to trees to be planted in memory of 30 men from the village who lost their lives during the First World War. Interestingly the names of the fallen had been placed in a

hat to decide whose name was to be on the special tree planted in the churchyard. Sidney Fountain's name was the one drawn out.

Most exciting of all, in the 5th November issue of the paper, a long article headed 'Trees as a Memorial to Fallen Comrades' stated clearly:

> 'Practical expression of the spirit of the British Legion was given by the members of the Tylers Green and Penn branch on Saturday when between thirty and forty ex-servicemen assembled on Tylers Green Common armed with picks, spades and forks, and planted trees which will be a memorial to fallen comrades, as well as a commemoration of Coronation year ... The trees chosen for the purpose are well-grown specimens of red-twigged lime, and they will be seen to advantage in various parts of the village.'

The article went on to give a detailed account of where in the village these groups of trees had been planted. Clearly there had never been an avenue, but 30 trees around the village.

The Reads now knew where and when the limes were planted and it seemed appropriate to try to identify the trees still in existence, to fill in any gaps with new trees and, with help, to restore this living memorial. A working group emerged, involving other local people: Miles Green, local historian, representing the Penn and Tylers Green Residents Society, Geoff Jones for the British Legion, Jeff Herschel for the Parish Council and Ron Saunders, who was coincidentally writing a book about the families of those local men who died during the First World War. Graeme Kirstie and his team from the Parish Council cleared away scrub that had established around some of the trees.

Following successful fundraising by the committee, seven new lime saplings were planted to replace the missing trees. The British Legion arranged for plaques to be made recording the details and place of death of each man.

The Special Trees and Woods Project provided an information board about the story of these now very special trees

Finally, a very moving re-dedication ceremony (shown opposite) organised by the British Legion was held on the Back Common on 28th June 2009, the 90th anniversary of the signing of the Treaty of Versailles which formally ended the First World War. It is hoped that the 30 trees will continue to be a fitting memorial to the men from this small village who did not return from the War.

As they stand today the 30 trees are mostly lime but there are some beeches. It may be that some of the original limes died and were replaced by beech. Or quite possibly the newspaper report (or the specimens selected) was not quite correct in the first place!

A rather sad postscript is that some of the newly planted trees and plaques were vandalised, but the overwhelming public support, moral and financial – including a touching contribution from children of Tylers Green First School – has been very heartening and has enabled the trees to be replaced, now with extra protection.

West of Hazlemere-Beaconsfield road in Tylers Green. Turn by the pond, then right at the crossroads by the pub and church into Church Road. The interpretation panel is approx 90m along the track runing west from the village hall. **Grid: SU904940**

Cliveden

Cliveden, originally built in 1664, is home to a large number of magnificent trees, the most famous of which is perhaps the Canning Oak. The tree was a favourite of Lord Canning, a frequent visitor who became Prime Minister in 1827. Canning is said to have spent hours seated beneath this tree enjoying spectacular views of the River Thames. Sadly the Canning Oak fell in 2004, almost 200 years after his visits, but its trunk is still there and the view remains breathtaking.

The Blenheim Pavilion at Cliveden, built to commemorate the Battle of Blenheim where, in 1704, the French were 'masterfully defeated' by the British, is still a major visitor attraction today. Less well known is the story that the Earl of Orkney, second in command to Lord Marlborough at the battle, also planted trees to reflect Marlborough's victorious battle order in the grounds at Cliveden which was his home at the time.

A 1749 map of the estate clearly shows trees in a most peculiar arrangement. There are five square sets of 16 trees each along the line of the higher ground. Was this the pattern used by the arch-tactician Marlborough at Blenheim? Finding proof on the ground is difficult, not least because the trees would be roughly 300 years old by now, but also because Cliveden's most notable owner, Lord Astor, remodelled the whole garden in the early 1900s. One rank does, however, survive within Cliveden's current boundaries and can be seen on the right where cars must slow for the inner entrance.

'Canning is said to have spent hours seated beneath this tree enjoying spectacular views of the River Thames'

'You can't walk by the river at Cliveden Reach and not believe in God.'

Sir Stanley Spencer

A long way from the sophisticated splendour of the house, a beautiful sycamore grows beside the boathouse. The tree stands at a towering 28m high, and has a girth of 6.4m. Although not a county champion, it is a great beauty and its unusually shaped branches add to its grandeur. The painter Sir Stanley Spencer, who spent most of his life in Cookham on the other side of the river, said of this area: 'You can't walk by the river at Cliveden Reach and not believe in God.'

A very peculiar tree can be found in the Gas Yard, an area built to accommodate wagons bringing in coal for the gas plant. The chimney was disguised as a tree trunk as part of Lord Astor's innovations of 1893 and is still fooling the casual observer today. The Chimney Tree can be found at the far end on the right, next to the weighbridge where fuel was delivered.

Cliveden is well signposted on the A4 Maidenhead-Slough and the A404 Maidenhead-High Wycombe. See the National Trust website for further information. A map of the grounds is available. **Grid: SU911855**

Near the statue of the Duke of Sutherland, in a place named the Half Moon, an unusual picnic spot can be found. Lord Astor wagered that a slab cut from a redwood could easily seat 40 people for dinner; thus a giant sequoia, that had lived its life a long way from the Chilterns, was imported to prove his point. Bringing it from North America cannot have been easy but positioning it on the slopes above the river would have been infinitely trickier. The cross-section has a circumference of over 15m and so seating 40 was indeed possible. Lord Astor won his bet, and his family are said to have enjoyed many a meal in the woods on their unique picnic table.

~

Cliveden is home to a fine collection of trees from all around the world. Some of the more unusual species include sassafras trees, a snowdrop tree and a handkerchief tree, a favourite tree of many of the volunteers.

Taplow Tulip

Two grand tulip trees adorn the grounds of what was once an Elizabethan Manor in Taplow; the current building dates back to Georgian times and is now the Taplow House Hotel.

Growing at the bottom of the lawn, the larger of the tulip trees is, at 35m high, the tallest tulip tree in the UK and Ireland.

On each tree a plaque proudly declares that Queen Elizabeth I herself may have planted it. Alas, there is one minor flaw in this proclamation. On the very same signs the date of planting is estimated to be 1770 to 1775.

History was clearly not a strong point of the signs' creator. Queen Elizabeth I reigned from 1558 until her death in 1603, 150 years earlier than the two trees are reported to have been planted and nearly 50 years before the first tulip tree was introduced to the UK in 1650! Unless there is some untold ghost story surrounding them, this royal connection seems likely to be no more than wishful thinking.

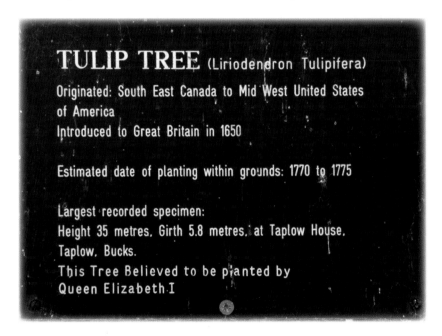

These trees are in the grounds of Taplow House Hotel on the southern edge of Taplow Village. From A4 (Maidenhead-Slough), turn into Cliveden Road. The hotel is on the right after approx a third of a mile. **Grid: SU909818**

The 'Greatest Ash'

When shown this 1930s photo of 'the greatest ash tree in England' (below) standing tall and proud in front of Chalfont Park, we just had to find out more about it. The tree was measured in 1860, when its girth was recorded as 7.62m.

Volunteer Graham accepted the challenge to investigate the 'greatest ash' further. He went to Chalfont Park and located the impressive tree with the aid of the photo. Graham measured the tree and confirmed that in the intervening years it has grown a little. The girth is now 8.41m.

However, after examining the leaves Graham realised the tree is not the 'greatest ash' in England but an American plane. Could it be that this tree has been mistaken for an ash for 150 years or was there originally an ash tree that died and was replaced by the plane?

This tree is on private land at Chalfont Park, but can be seen from the road (A413, about two miles from the junction with the A40 near Gerrards Cross).
Grid: TQ008895

Remnantz Walnut

Now showing signs of great age this tree is taller than the recorded UK champion black walnut. Significant numbers of this North American tree were imported after 1709. A harsh winter in Europe that year damaged so many walnut trees that a ban was imposed on the export of timber to Britain. The market in walnut was dominated by the French and, at that time, France was at war with Britain (the War of the Spanish Succession). As walnut timber was highly valued for its weight, strength and resistance to splitting, another source was needed and the Americas had the answer.

During the American Civil War 'to shoulder walnut' meant to enlist in the army, gun stocks being made of walnut. By the Second World War the phrase had altered its meaning and referred to starting an aeroplane as propellers then were made from walnut.

These are not the only military connections of this tree which grows in the former grounds of Remnantz in Marlow. This grand house was the first home of the Royal Military College which is now at Sandhurst.

An early 19th century painting (above) of the College's Junior Department on parade before the Duke of York at Remnantz appears to show this tree on the extreme right. The location matches perfectly and the size and shape are spot on for a young walnut tree.

'This tree is taller than the recorded UK champion black walnut'

After the days of the College, Remnantz was bought by Thomas Wethered, brewer of the town. From that point he was known about the town as the Squire not the Brewer, just by virtue of buying the house! The Wethered family sold Remnantz a few years ago and, pleasingly, the new 'Squire', Steven Bosley, is a military auctioneer.

This tree is in a private garden. There is a plaque on an old gate post on the A4155 Marlow-Henley-on-Thames road opposite Shelley Cottage, near Sir William Borlase's Grammar School. **Grid: SU846863**

Sparky's Ash

Clyde 'Sparky' Cosper saved the town of Princes Risborough on 13th November 1943.

The B-17 Sparky was flying was on course to crash directly on the town. 26 year old Sparky bravely remained at the controls, managing to clear the rooftops and crash in a field well clear of the town. The full bomb load exploded on impact and the plane was blown to pieces.

'Miriam', the B17's nose name, had taken off earlier with its crew of ten and was waiting for the other planes in the flight to join it. Their mission was to bomb German U-boat berths at Bremen. The weather was bad, the take-off was dicey and the climb for altitude was worse. The plane flew into a thunderstorm and the downdraft threw it into an abrupt dive. Sparky ordered the crew to bale out and the nine other men came down bruised, but alive.

A plaque marking Sparky's bravery and sacrifice is outside the library in Princes Risborough. In 1993, an ash tree was planted there to add to the memorial, though the library is not the crash site.

This memorial is to honour those young people of this District conscripted for National Service from 1945 until 1963

They served in all the Nations Armed Forces in search of some peace some only finding death on active service

Long may their contribution be appreciated

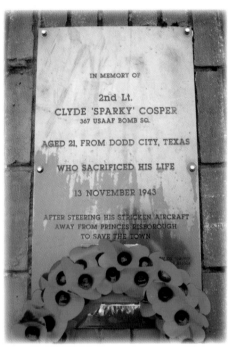

IN MEMORY OF

2nd Lt.
CLYDE 'SPARKY' COSPER
367 USAAF BOMB SQ.

AGED 21, FROM DODD CITY, TEXAS

WHO SACRIFICED HIS LIFE

13 NOVEMBER 1943

AFTER STEERING HIS STRICKEN AIRCRAFT
AWAY FROM PRINCES RISBOROUGH
TO SAVE THE TOWN

The tree is in front of the library in the centre of Princes Risborough (A4010).
Grid: SP808034

Pullingshill Wood

Pullingshill Wood is a quiet and peaceful spot renowned for the First World War practice trenches which can be found on site. They are a very well preserved example of this feature in the UK and were built by various regiments (including the Grenadier Guards) stationed nearby at Bovingdon Green during 1915 and 1916.

The trenches are in good condition and their pattern can be followed today despite natural infilling through soil and leaf litter build-up. Local group Archaeology in Marlow recently researched the history of the trenches in a Lottery-funded project – two interpretation panels on the site help to document trenches which run for over 1,400m through the wood.

First World War trenches

An ancient sloping wood bank divides the wood from the common and is the boundary between Medmenham Parish and Great Marlow Parish. It is believed that this dates back to the Norman Conquest.

The wood also has more recent claims to fame; in 1996 it featured in the film *101 Dalmatians*. Although the woods put in a sterling performance, the weather did not, and snow machines had to be brought in to give the wintry weather the script called for.

At the west side of Marlow, turn north-west by Platts Garage (A4155) towards Frieth. Half a mile to the north of Bovingdon Green turn south-west to Marlow Common and Wood.
Grid: SU822865 - Pullingshill Wood; SU825872 – Marlow Common

Among the other sights to see if you visit this wood is a huge, coppiced sweet chestnut tree on the slope. The tree was felled in about 1914 when the area was used by training troops in preparation for the fighting on the continent. Since then it has re-grown to a massive size, with seven new trunks.

Special tree volunteer and local artist June Kingsbury has fond memories of climbing in the tree over 30 years ago when she and her friends named this landmark tree 'Seven Sisters' (see also front cover image).

Other striking mature trees are scattered throughout the woods. Many of these unfortunately suffered from storms during 1987 and 1990. The wood has been designated a Site of Special Scientific Interest and, together with part of the adjoining Marlow Common, is now owned by the Woodland Trust.

The woods' history and location (the Chiltern Way cuts through them), make it a very popular area with walkers.

Early September evening by Keith Beckett-Hester

Pulpit Hill

Pulpit Hill is a promontory of the Chiltern Hills located about two miles north-east of Princes Risborough. There is a steep escarpment on the north-west side of the hill, overlooking the Vale of Aylesbury, and the south-west flank is a steep slope. It is quite flat on top, at a height of 240m, and the land slopes gradually away towards the east. The hill is of Cretaceous chalk capped with clay and flint. Pulpit Wood covers the hilltop, the escarpment and slope and it came into the ownership of the National Trust in 1985. Previously this area had been part of the Hampden estate which has a history going back to the 11th century. The woodland is mostly of beech but has stands of conifers – Norway spruce, western red cedar, Corsican pine and larch – which were planted before the National Trust took over the management. Other hard woods include oak, ash and sycamore. Where mature trees have died or clearings appeared ash saplings are prevalent.

Some of the finest beech trees are to be found on the summit and in amongst the trees are the double ramparts of an ancient hill fort which can be clearly seen today. With its prominent position, Pulpit Hill must have been an important stronghold and look-out post and the fort dates back to the Iron Age. Some pieces of pottery have been found at the site which date from about 400 BC. Other finds include flint flakes of Neolithic origin (about 2000 BC) suggesting there may have been settlements there for a very long period of time. People living there may even have had a water supply, as the clay cap can retain water and today a small permanent dew-pond exists to the east of the fort. It seems likely that the hilltop was bare of trees in ancient times so it is difficult to imagine what it must have looked like.

More recently, old maps show that woodland extended over the hilltop in the early 19th century but that the south-west flank was pasture and scrubland. The woodland would have provided firewood, timber for

Pulpit Hill by Judy Nash

building, and also livestock grazing. Soon after 1800 Kimble Parish boundary enclosed the wood and the spot was marked by a long bank planted with beech trees. Today the path leading to the hill fort follows this line and in fact the bank can be traced right across the fort in the south-west corner.

Later in the 19th century the furniture industry began to flourish in High Wycombe and beech trees were planted throughout the Chilterns to provide the wood. Pulpit Hill was no exception and many of the mature beech trees standing today were probably planted at that time. At various points in the wood saw pits bear witness to this industry.

Pulpit Wood shows the marks of its history but today the area is actively managed in the long term in order to improve the woodland, encourage the spread of chalk grassland on the south-west slope and preserve the hill fort (which is listed as a Scheduled Ancient Monument). In the short term, when trees die they are left standing where possible, and when they fall they are left to rot on the ground to enhance the biodiversity. Where trees grow densely together, thinning is sometimes carried out. Adjacent to Pulpit Wood is the Grangelands Site of Special Scientific Interest and part of the south-west slope is included in this area. Some rare plants are known to grow here, in particular the bird's nest orchid and species of helleborine. These plants require shady woodland if they are to survive so an important aspect of the woodland management is to maintain this habitat on the slope.

Pulpit Wood is popular with walkers and several paths cross the area. There is easy access from a small car park just above Cadsden.

From A4010 High Wycombe-Aylesbury road, turn south-east at the Askett roundabout into Cadsden Road. Drive uphill for approx one and a quarter miles to a car park on the left.
Grid: SP833045

'The history of Penn Wood can be traced back to Roman times'

Penn Wood

The history of Penn Wood, one of the largest ancient woodlands in the Chilterns, can be traced back to Roman times. Its name derives from the Old English term for enclosure or pen and dates back to when the area was a deer enclosure during Anglo-Saxon times. The area was such a feature of the surrounding landscape that it gave its name to the wood and nearby village.

From before the Norman Conquest until the mid-19th century, Penn Wood was part of a very large area of wood pasture common. When the wood was enclosed in 1855 most was awarded to Earl Howe. Much of the timber had been felled in anticipation of the removal of commoners' rights and Earl Howe converted his new land to high forest. At this time the rides were created for the Countess who was fond of driving in the woods. She particularly enjoyed the ornamental varieties of rhododendron, azalea, cherry laurel and conifers planted for her benefit.

Evidence of former industry and activity still remains, with archaeological features across the site such as wood banks, flint and clay pits. In 1800 the wood from the site was a source of legs, stretchers, spindles and sticks for Windsor and cane-backed chairs. Many bodgers working in Penn Wood supplied this thriving industry. The chair-manufacturing firm Dancer & Hearne started up in a shed behind the Hit or Miss Pub in Penn Street.

'These two panels show the effects of light and weather conditions on the landscape, portraying the power of nature and the beauty of trees and the elements.'
                    Patricia Lynch

Woodland Variations by Patricia Lynch

In 1993 The Committee of the Friends of Penn Wood was formed in response to a threat of a golf course being constructed in the wood. After a long campaign led by the Friends of Penn Wood, with the help of the local community and local organisations, the Secretary of State refused permission for the development. The owner then advertised the wood for sale in small lots. This time the Friends of Penn Wood campaigned to buy the wood. Following successful local fund raising, a considerable grant from the Heritage Lottery Fund and the support the Woodland Trust, the Wood's future was secured.

Today Penn Wood is a very varied site including many different habitats such as high forest, conifer plantation, acid grassland, rhododendron avenues and ponds. Among the woodland and areas of natural regeneration some old growth features survive including one veteran oak and the remains of an ancient collapsed beech tree. There is a scattering of trees over 200 years old across the site, remnants from the days when it was a wood pasture.

'It is an ancient woodland with an ancient oak at its heart ... this ancient stumpy and hollow tree became the meeting place for artists and musicians, families and friends.'

Isabel Fallow

By the A404 Amersham-High Wycombe road. Turn south to Penn Street and park in the village near the pub. **Grid: SU924963**

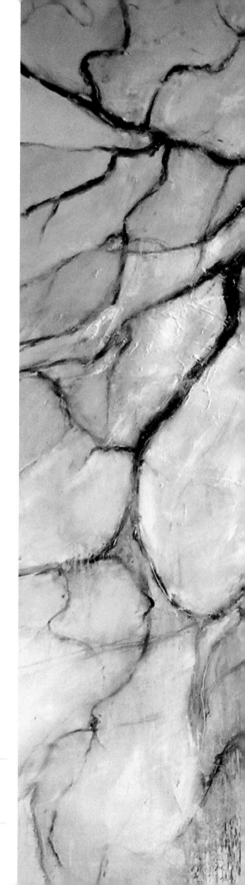

Under the Ancient Oak by Isabel Fallow

Hodgemoor Wood

Today, most people think of Hodgemoor Woods as a pleasant place to walk or ride their horses. What many people may not realise is that Hodgemoor is an ancient woodland and is one of the largest tracts of semi-natural woodlands remaining in the Buckinghamshire Chilterns.

The earliest record of the wood dates back to the 13th century but there has been considerable fluctuation in the extent of the wood, so that the ancient core is surrounded by semi-natural woodland dating from the 18th century and more recently. The wood is situated on an unusually large range of soil types and supports a wide range of woodland vegetation and flowering plants characteristic of the Chilterns, as well as others which are more uncommon in Buckinghamshire. Not surprisingly, important populations of insects, including the rare jewel beetle, can be found in the wood. The wood was designated as a Site of Special Scientific Interest in 1992.

The wood lies in the parishes of Coleshill and Seer Green, with the part in Coleshill made up of three separate woods; Hales Wood, Highfield Grove and Hill Wood. The most ancient part of the wood however, the area that is actually called Hodgemoor, lies in Seer Green which, until 1847, belonged to the parish of Farnham Royal. The fact that Hodgemoor lies in two separate parishes suggests that different parts of the wood were once owned by different people, and may give some clue as to the different ages of the wood.

Reprint of the first edition of the Ordnance Survey map of England and Wales, sheet 71: London & Windsor

Records show that High Wood, Hales Wood and Highfield Grove all belonged to the Tyrrwhit-Drake family who owned the Shardeloes Estate, then in the parish of Coleshill. The land was heavy clay and thus not suitable for agriculture. However, there are records for the 200 years up to 1850 showing that the land was used for timber. Such a history explains why the trees there today are of a more recent origin, rather than ancient woodland.

In 1939, Buckinghamshire County Council paid £6,269 for a parcel of 63.4 hectares of land, the title deeds of which reveal that it came from three separate sources: a piece of farmland in the south-east corner belonging to the glebe lands in Seer Green; a small area in the top north-east corner which included four small dwellings; and finally, Hodgemoor Wood itself.

Of the four dwellings – Maisie's Cottage, the Pest House and 1 and 2 Froghall Cottages – Masie's Cottage is the only one which still exists and is inhabited, a pretty house on Bottrells Lane which runs through Hodgemoor. Little remains of the Pest House although it lingers in the memories of older inhabitants of the village who say it is where sufferers of the plague were sent. No sign of Froghall Cottages remains, although the name is known locally.

An entry in the Domesday Book may reveal why Hodgemoor's core of ancient woodland has been so well preserved, and even holds a clue to its name. In 1086, Bertram of Verdun, lord of the manor of Farnham Royal, had an area of woodland in Amersham where he kept 600 pigs. Sometime around the beginning of the 17th century the wood, then known as Hoggemoor, was granted to a William Waad Esq by Queen Elizabeth I. As 'Hogge' is an old variation of the word 'hog', it is thought that the area was kept as grazing for pigs, and thus outlasted the more modern woodland which surrounds it.

As well as providing us with a link to the past, Hodgemoor played an important role in more recent history. There are many Polish families who remember Hodgemoor as a safe home after the war and, near the car park, there is a monument commemorating the Polish War Camp. From 1947 until 1962, the area was full of temporary buildings, barracks buildings and Nissen huts and was home to 156 Polish families. These were mainly the families of Polish servicemen from the Third Carpathian division in Italy who could not safely return to Poland. Conditions in the camp were basic but all necessary amenities were provided and it was a proper community with a Church, an infant school, a post office, a shop and an entertainment hall.

To east of A355 Beaconsfield-Amersham road. There is a car park approx one mile along Bottrells Lane on right hand side. Entrance to Bottrells Lane lies behind the lay-by opposite the Magpies Public House. **Grid: SU 965937**

More recently still, local families share memories of:

> ' ... running through dry beech leaves in some mysterious dells in the middle of the wood. Other children would ride their bicycles up and down the slopes of the dells or swing over them from ropes slung from branches of trees. At the time, the area seemed like a natural children's playground but ... it was perhaps the remnants of diggings for clay to be used in the local brick kilns.'

Whilst the generation before that spent 'long days in [their] childhood playing in the woods and building "cubbies" in the bracken ... collect[ing] firewood which they sold for tuppence a load'.

Hodgemoor undoubtedly has a varied and interesting history. It remains today as an important resource to be enjoyed, remembered and cherished in many ways by many different people.

Queen Elizabeth Oak

This ancient tree would have already been a large, impressive specimen in the 16th century, during Queen Elizabeth's reign. It is now known as the Queen Elizabeth Oak because she is said to have lost some jewellery beneath it during a stay at Chenies Manor House. But is this story fact or fiction?

Research by volunteers at the Bedford and Luton Archives and Records Service confirmed that Queen Elizabeth visited Chenies with her entourage on several occasions. According to an entry in a wardrobe book, she did indeed lose some jewellery, tiny gold fastenings called aglets, whilst there in 1570; 'Item – lost from the face of a gown, in our wearing the same at Cheynes, July anno 12 (1570), one pair of small aglets, enamelled blue, parcel of 183 pair'. This is quoted in Strickland, *Lives of the Queens of England*, Vol V1, pp.279-280. He goes on to say:

> *'The aglets were the ornamental loops of goldsmiths' work with which all Elizabeth's robes, according to the portraits, were very thickly besprinkled. In this case there were no less than a hundred and eighty-three pairs. The aglets were movable and were changed from one dress to another.'*

Given the size and considerable number of aglets on an elaborate costume it is likely that any loss would be discovered too late to establish exactly where it occurred.

In her book Family Background (1949), Gladys Scott Thomson may have fuelled the legend that the loss occurred whilst the queen was sitting under the ancient oak. She writes:

> 'One thing … upon which the Queen must have looked has survived to the present day. It is a magnificent but very old oak tree. That it must have been a flourishing growth in 1570 disposes of the other tradition … that it was planted by Elizabeth in commemoration of the visit.'

She goes straight on to mention the loss of the aglets, perhaps encouraging readers to infer that the loss occurred in the vicinity of the tree.

There was a reference in the woods accounts, part of the household accounts, written by a steward of the estate in the 1830s which explains that the policy towards the woods was to 'save all the best and finest trees and only to fell the worst and most indifferent'. Perhaps this is one reason why the old oak continued to survive even when the policy became more commercial after 1831. The tree has attracted much attention over the years and its image has been reproduced in numerous books, postcards and paintings.

Henry Moule was a prolific 19th century artist. He often painted the landscape around Dorchester, providing a unique record of the Victorian countryside. He was the first curator of the Dorset County Museum which now exhibits many Moule watercolours. Moule also painted in Buckinghamshire and the Queen Elizabeth Oak features in a picture entitled Palace House at Chenies (below).

Palace House at Chenies by Henry Moule

The Manor House in the centre of Chenies village is open to the public between April and October – please check for opening hours and admission prices. North of A404, halfway between the M25 and Chalfont. **Grid: TQ016983**

Fawley Court

Sir Christopher Wren designed Fawley Court in the 17th century and the grounds, laid out by Capability Brown, give lovely vistas in several directions. It is said that in 1731 every kind of tree known in Europe was planted here. The once large estate has diminished over the centuries but the grounds still contain many beautiful trees including a cucumber tree, a tulip tree, a fern-leafed beech and incense cedars.

Fawley Court was re-modelled by the English architect James Wyatt in the late 18th century. At the same time a folly on an island in the Thames was built as a fishing lodge for Sambrooke Freeman, Fawley Court's owner. The folly, which is known as the Temple and gave the island its name, completed a view from the house through an avenue of lime trees.

On the island itself there are a number of trees, the most impressive being the weeping beech tree which measures 2.5m in girth (see below).

Fawley Court is connected to another estate about a mile upstream, Phyllis Court, by a magnificent avenue of 121 large London plane trees. Sadly, the avenue is no longer in the ownership of either estate, but it can be admired from a public footpath.

One mile north-east of Henley-on-Thames on A4155 Henley-Marlow road. All three estates are in private ownership but limited access to Phyllis Court and Greenlands may be arranged by telephoning 01491 570500 and 01491 571454 respectively.

Phyllis Court (above) is on the edge of Henley-on-Thames, situated near the finishing post of the Henley Royal Regatta course, and is now a private members' country club. Many of the specimen trees in the gardens, including a wellingtonia, holm oak and weeping ash, can be seen from the towpath on the other side of the river.

A little further in the opposite direction is Greenlands, which since 1946 has been the site of the Henley Business School, now part of the University of Reading. Established on an ancient site, the 19th century house was home to W H Smith, who founded the chain of newsagents which bears his name. Many of the special trees in the grounds of Greenlands, including a swamp cypress and the long, beautifully shaped yew hedge, can also be seen from the towpath on the other side of the Thames.

One of the smallest special trees in the Chilterns is found within the grounds of the Henley Business School. It is an olive tree planted by Archbishop Desmond Tutu in May 2006 to celebrate the opening of the Tutu Peace Garden.

These three neighbouring estates, linked by the River Thames and 700 years of English history, have been transformed over the centuries. Today they stand as a reminder of regicide, restoration, agricultural and industrial revolutions which changed the landscape and the trees that shaped it.

All three estates can be seen from the Thames Path on the Berkshire bank of the river. In addition, a public footpath runs east along the boundary of Phyllis Court from the A4155 to the Thames and then north along the river bank through Fawley Court to the edge of the Greenlands estate.

Bottom Wood

This ancient semi-natural woodland is owned by the Chiltern Society. Since receiving the wood as a donation from Mrs Cynthia Ercolani in 1984 it has been managed as a nature reserve.

It flourishes with bluebells and other woodland flowers in the spring, and is a good place to see red kites and other birds of prey. The wood was heavily felled of its better timber in 1940 as part of the war effort and has since re-grown with a wide range of native broadleaved trees.

The ancient wood covers 11.5 hectares and an area known as Toothill (below) covers a further three hectares, where conifers and beech were planted by local scouts in 1951. Part of Toothill is now managed as a chalk grassland glade for wild flowers and butterflies, and common dormice are found in the adjoining scrub.

Bottom Wood contains many archaeological features including strip lynchets of a once farmed terraced hillside which was abandoned hundreds of years ago; numerous sawpits and a hollow-way to an old well used during a drought in the 1920s. The well is now capped in concrete.

The wood is now managed by the Chiltern Woodlands Project and volunteers from the Chiltern Society's Bottom Wood Group.

One of the many sawpits at Bottom Wood

Park at the top end of the Old Dashwood Hill near the junction with the A40 at Studley Green south of Stokenchurch; follow the bridleway down the hill to find Bottom Wood in the valley bottom. **Grid: SU797955**

Hertfordshire

WOODS OF THE WHIPPENDELL VALLEY

ASHRIDGE

WAR WOUNDS

HOCKERIDGE AND PANCAKE WOODS

ABBEY PAGODA

DOMESDAY OAK

CROXLEY GREEN'S COMMEMORATIVE TREES

Woods of the Whippendell Valley

Between Watford, Croxley Green and the M25 lie over 130 hectares of contiguous woodland, much of which is open to the public and within walking distance of the London Underground. It is mostly ancient, semi-natural woodland with wonderful displays of bluebells and cherry blossom in spring.

The woods lie between the chalk streams of the Gade and the Chess at the south-eastern edge of the Chilterns, where the hills meet the Colne valley. They comprise Harrocks Wood, Jacotts Hill (previously the Upper Park of Cassiobury Mansion), Whippendell Wood and Lees Wood, now used as an outdoor centre. Linking all these woodlands is the Whippendell dry valley which runs roughly north to south. Many years ago this valley was formed by streams as the ice age glaciers melted. It makes an attractive central feature in Whippendell wood and marks the steep western edge of Lees Wood and Jacotts Hill.

The woodland landscape has been shaped by human activity over the centuries. In medieval times, the land was owned by St Alban's Abbey and there are remains of some small buildings in Lees Wood which are thought to go back to those days. The story goes that several cells were built there as a place of punishment for monks who had misbehaved. Later, the woods were divided between the Cassiobury, Clarendon and Redheath estates and they were used for hunting as well as firewood and timber. There is plenty of evidence of coppicing.

HARROCKS WOOD

Many trees in Harrocks Wood are relatively young due to the timber extraction which took place before the Woodland Trust took ownership in 1986. There is a lot of birch, ash and hazel in this wood, however larger beech and oaks survive on the margins and sweet chestnuts and sycamores within the woods themselves.

Harrocks Wood (including Merlin's Dell and Newlands Spring) was originally part of the Redheath estate which, from 1709 until 1922, was owned by the Finch family. Dury and Andrew's 1766 map of Hertford-shire shows that the wooded area of the estate was a good deal larger than today. Merlin's Wood stretched much further west towards the house and south to the edge of Croxley Green. By the 19th century however, trees had been replaced by fields and the wood boundaries were much as they are today.

At the same time as they were reducing the woods, the Finch family was known for planting ornamental trees around the house. In Victorian times 'Finch's Avenue' was a local landmark. At the Clarendon Arms (in Chandlers Cross) one could obtain:

> 'Good accommodation for your horse while you walk across a field to the left, the path through which leads to Finch's Avenue, a splendidly shady promenade half a mile or so in length, under beech trees of immense height and fine growth… the picturesqueness of which is greatly enhanced by the view in the distance of Mr Finch's mansion.'

It was said of it that 'there are finer individual trees elsewhere but nowhere else in the country is there a beech avenue of such length and beauty'. The Clarendon Arms is still there, although dining rather than stabling horses is their speciality nowadays. The avenue survives too as a fine ride through Harrocks Wood and some rotted stumps of the original beeches can still be seen beside the path.

JACOTTS HILL

The jewel of Jacotts Hill is the ancient lime avenue which runs from the River Gade to Whippendell Wood. Cassiobury was the family seat of the Capels for over 250 years until 1922. Arthur Capel, a staunch supporter of Charles I, was beheaded in 1649. After the restoration of the monarchy, his son was created Earl of Essex, and celebrated with an extensive rebuilding of Cassiobury House, and the laying out of spectacular formal gardens. The lime avenue was planted as a feature of the deer park in about 1720.

'A fine day at Cassiobury comes within measurable distance of heaven'

Also dating from the 18th century, there was a second avenue of elms on Jacotts Hill, crossing the limes from north to south. For many years they ornamented the golf course after the West Herts Golf Club took on the lease in 1897, reaching as far as the first tee by the club house. One of the trees was responsible for a tragedy in 1923. Bystanders heard a sudden crack as a limb broke but the player, Mr Osborne, who was concentrating on his shot, took the full force of the falling branch and was killed. In the 1960s the elms succumbed to disease, and since then the Club has replanted the central part of the course. In amongst the new young trees, where the public footpath from Redheath crosses to Ironbridge Lock, there are some ancient limes that mark the site of the old Lodge, home of the Earl's park keeper. Jacotts Hill is now a good deal more wooded than it was a hundred years ago and the Club is justly proud of the beauty of its course.

WHIPPENDELL WOOD

Whippendell Wood, which formed part of the Cassiobury estate, has similarly been transformed over the years. The northern part was replanted with broadleaf trees and some larches in the 1960s and 1970s, but there are more mature trees in the southern section including oak standards with hazel coppice beneath and some fine beeches. It is perhaps the most varied of the woods and is a Site of Special Scientific Interest due to the large area of semi-natural vegetation, the rich variety of fungi and the invertebrate fauna. As well as bluebells in the spring, the woods contain a wide variety of plant species, one of the more unusual being the coralroot bittercress (a relative of the lady's smock).

LEES WOOD

The remaining part of the woodland mosaic, Lees Wood, was part of the Clarendon estate until the early years of the 20th century. It is the most distinct of the group since much of the wood is planted with pines, a legacy of the Forestry Commission from around 1960. The earlier landscape was probably mature oak trees with hazel coppice beneath, as is found in the neighbouring Lord Hyde campsite.

Lees Wood is visited every year by Scouts and Guides from far and wide. They enjoy a range of outdoor activities, including a 10m climbing wall, an assault course and a rifle range. In future, the Scouts plan to return the woodland closer to its traditional aspect by replanting the pines with native broadleaf trees.

~

All told, the collection of woods between Watford, Croxley Green and Chandlers Cross is a haven for wildlife and a wonderful asset for recreation. Whether admiring the sea of blue flowers under the April trees in Merlin's Wood or walking in the frosty sun slanting through Whippendell on a winter's day, this is a splendid place to be. West Herts Golf Course quotes Bernard Darwin in 1910:

'A fine day at Cassiobury comes within measurable distance of heaven.'

Applied to the woodland as a whole, who could disagree?

Half a mile south-east of Chandler's Cross along minor road. Approaches: north from A412 at Croxley Green church; west from A411 near M25 roundabout.
Grid: TQ076976

Ashridge

Throughout the wooded areas of the Ashridge Estate there are many veteran and ancient trees which are largely accessible to visitors. There is much standing and fallen dead wood which is left to support a very rich variety of insects and other wildlife. The estate is nationally important for wildlife conservation and includes a very large Site of Special Scientific Interest.

Today the Ashridge estate is owned by the National Trust and covers 2,000 hectares, of which 910 hectares is woodland, together with commons, chalk grassland and farmland. The Chiltern escarpment above Aldbury is heavily wooded. There are also many special trees in the gardens of Ashridge House (opposite), which is in separate ownership.

The archaeology of the Ashridge estate shows continuous occupation from pre-Roman times. There are tumuli, pillow mounds by the Monument and Romano-British field systems. Ancient hollow-ways mark the routes taken by generations of villagers from the clay vale below, driving livestock to the commons on the hills or bringing down fuel.

The documented history of the Ashridge estate began when Edmund, Earl of Cornwall, nephew of Henry III, endowed a monastery, the College of Bonhommes, in 1283. Edmund's father held the royal manor and castle of Berkhamsted where Edmund was born in 1249. Edmund gave his new foundation a portion of a relic of the Sacred Blood of Jesus which attracted pilgrims to Ashridge. The rights given to the College included 'pasturage in our woods of Berkhamsted, called the Frith, and putting their pigs into the same wood'.

Ashridge was acquired by the Egerton family in 1604. The Egertons had substantial land holdings elsewhere, including in the north-west where mines and canals later played a significant role in the family's fortunes. After being a senior statesman for Queen Elizabeth I, under James I
Sir Thomas Egerton became Lord Chancellor, and a Baron. Following his death in 1617 his son rapidly acquired an earldom, it is said with the help of a payment of £20,000, and became the first Earl of Bridgewater.

'This ancient house ... hath here a park for fallow and another for red deer, and in them especially near his house some lofty groves of trees and so thickset together that the like is scarce anywhere to be seen ... here are [red] squirrels in plenty which leap and dance from tree to tree.'

The second Earl of Ashridge

The deer parks were kept separate from other parts of the estate by carefully tended fences, left open in places as deer leaps, which allowed deer to enter the park but not escape.

In 1823 the future Queen Victoria, then aged four, visited Ashridge with her mother, the Duchess of Kent. During her visit she planted an oak tree on the south lawn, which has grown to become a fine and still healthy tree with a girth of 4.8m, known as Queen Victoria's Oak (below).

Francis, the eighth and last Earl of Bridgewater, died in 1829, leaving the sum of £13,500 and the design for an obelisk to commemorate the third Duke. His sister-in-law disliked the design so much that she insisted on it being built well away from the house and so the Monument, the modern symbol of Ashridge, was constructed on the edge of the escarpment overlooking Aldbury. Built in 1832 it is 33m high, with 170 steps to the viewing platform; from here there are magnificent views in all directions.

After the death of the eighth Earl the estate eventually passed to the Earls of Brownlow. The former commons of Pitstone and Ivinghoe were enclosed under Brownlow ownership without recorded incident. However, in 1866 a famous event took place on Berkhamsted Common; the second Earl Brownlow had fenced part of the Common and Augustus Smith, MP and owner of a house nearby, objected strongly to the loss of the common land and commoners' rights.

Helped by Britain's oldest national conservation body, the Commons Preservation Society, which was founded in the previous year (now called the Open Spaces Society), Augustus Smith sent 120 navvies by train to Tring, from where they walked up to the Common and pulled down all the fencing overnight. Legal disputes followed but the Common was never again fenced.

Autumn Woodland by Jackie Carden

The third Earl Brownlow inherited Ashridge, in 1867. When he died in 1921 his will directed that the Ashridge Estate should be sold; this was the first sale of the estate since 1604. Concerns were expressed over possible large-scale felling of trees, to be replaced with houses. Almost immediately the National Trust received an anonymous offer of £20,000 to buy part of the estate. Eventually a letter in *The Times* on 20th October 1925 signed by the Prime Minister Stanley Baldwin and others, including Ramsey Macdonald, called for the parkland to be acquired for the National Trust. The resulting public appeal raised over £40,000, enough for the Trust to buy 688 hectares. A year later the Trust was able to acquire another 67 hectares, including Frithsden Beeches.

'In all seasons it is beautiful here and a delight to paint and walk in or just come for a picnic - and to see the deer.'

Jackie Carden

Meanwhile the remainder of the estate was sold and in 1928 the house and 32 hectares were bought and presented to the Conservative Party. It was named the Bonar Law Memorial College, after Andrew Bonar Law who was briefly Prime Minister in 1922-23. During the Second World War the house was a hospital, with concrete buildings used as wards built in the grounds. Since this period the buildings have been used variously as a teachers' training college, part of the Public Record Office (until it relocated to Kew in 1978) and then a finishing school between 1949 and 1958. Since 1959 the house has been home to the Ashridge Management College, now known as the Ashridge Business School.

Ashridge gardens are open to the public at weekends in the summer and cover 77 hectares. In 1813 Humphry Repton was invited to design the 'pleasure garden' near to the house. The gardens comprise a number of Repton's original features, as well as a large lawn leading to avenues and groupings of trees. The avenue of Wellingtonias, planted only a few years after it was introduced to Britain in 1853, is an impressive sight. There is also a circle of Incense Cedars and some huge Sweet Chestnuts, thought originally to have been planted in a formation to represent the troops of an 18th century battle. Among the many features of interest within the estate the following are worthy of special mention:

~

The Golden Valley (shown on page 114) lies just beyond the Ashridge garden boundary and was originally landscaped by Lancelot 'Capability' Brown in around 1760. Bordered by attractive woodland the bottom of this dry dip slope valley is open grassland ideal for walking and picnics.

~

Frithsden Beeches nearby (below) was an area of wood-pasture by Berkhamsted Common and today is a stand of ancient pollard beeches with bollings (pollard trunks) up to 1.5m in diameter. Believed to have been last pollarded between 1820 and 1850, they have developed crowns up to 36m in diameter. The area has featured in films such as *Harry Potter*, on TV in programmes such as *Jonathan Creek* and in advertisements, earning valuable funds for the National Trust.

'It is possible to walk for several miles through Ashridge without having to cross a fence, perhaps the nearest thing to a wilderness experience to be found in the Home Counties.'

Frithsden Great and Little Copse lie on the south-western side of the Frithsden Valley and to the south of Ashridge house. According to Oliver Rackham they were originally embanked coppice woods which lay adjacent to Berkhamsted Common, although the Great Copse has been substantially replanted. The banks would have been topped by temporary fencing to exclude grazing livestock after the underwood had been coppiced, until the regrowth had grown above the height reached by grazing animals. Little Copse today contains a mixture of species including hornbeam, cherry, chestnut and field maple, with standard trees of oak and beech, but no beech in the underwood, representing, Rackham says, a rare survival of the medieval Chiltern woodland landscape.

~

In the 13th century Berkhamsted Frith was a wooded common of 526 hectares, probably the largest in the Chilterns. These areas would have been grazed and wood taken for fuel. While the copses retained the variety of species described above, the wood-pasture in Frithsden Beeches became pure beech. In contrast, where grazing has recently stopped the area has been colonised by birch and oak.

The Candelabra Tree (right) looks like an old-fashioned candle holder, and was formerly part of a hedge, possibly alongside one of the hollow ways running up the escarpment.

The Big Boundary Oak (left) is one of a series of trees marking an old boundary, possibly between Buckinghamshire and Hertfordshire. The tree is clearly very ancient, as is shown by its colossal 6m circumference, and a large boundary oak is marked where it stands on a map from 1762.

The Ashridge Estate is on the Herts and Bucks border, between Aylesbury and Hemel Hempstead, three miles north of A41 between Tring and Berkhamstead, off B4506 from Northchurch (to Ringshall and Dagnall), or off the A489 from Dunstable.

War Wounds

During the Second World War American troops were based at the Ashridge Estate near Berkhamsted. Two months before D-Day some young soldiers recorded their stay in England by carving into a mature beech tree.

They engraved their home states - Texas, Tennessee, Virginia, North Carolina, Michigan, New York, Illinois and South Dakota - and the date, 4.5.44. In the States it is customary to write the month, the day and then the year so the date is thought to be 5th April 1944, rather than 4th May 1944. The engraving is topped by a 'V' for victory and followed by '. . . –' which is 'V' in Morse Code.

Bob Davis, the Head Forester for the National Trust, said:

> 'It is quite humbling to think these frightened young men, a long way from home, would soon be facing the horrors of the Normandy Landings which commenced on Tuesday 6th June 1944, D-Day.'

This tree grows in Thunderdell Wood which is owned by the National Trust. Public access is permitted at any time. To visit the tree, from the B4506 walk about 350m down Thunderdell Lane towards Ashridge house. When you see the open fields on your right, follow the fence line away from the lane. The tree is a couple of hundred metres along the fence line.

Park in National Trust Bridgewater Monument car park. Cross B4506; walk along Prince's Riding for approx half a mile. Turn right along signposted trail south for approx half a mile. The tree is on the right. **Grid: SP982122**

V

TENN
VA
NC
MICH
NY
IL
SD

4-5-44

Hockeridge and Pancake Woods

Hockeridge and Pancake Woods cover some 74 hectares south of Berkhamsted and are a fine example of native woodland mixed with over 50 species of non-native conifers.

Back in the 18th century the woods were owned and managed by the Dorrien family who lived nearby at Haresfoot House. Timber records from the 1790s show that they generated an annual income of up to £1,400 by selling oak, beech and other native trees. The family continued to own and manage the woods until the owner, Horace Smith Dorrien, a much decorated soldier, died in a road accident in 1930 and the estate was broken up. The Ashlyns estate was sold to the Foundling Hospital which was looking to move out of polluted London to the countryside. In 1944 the hospital purchased the woods 'to prevent them from falling into the hands of speculators who may get a poor class of house erected on them'.

Soon afterwards the Foundling Hospital went into decline and the woods were sold in 1952 to Miss Mary Wellesley, a descendant of the Duke of Wellington and a keen arboriculturalist. She rescued them from neglect and planted the many conifers still seen today. In 1986 Miss Wellesley handed the restored woods to the current owners, the Royal Forestry Society.

It is thanks to the far-sightedness of the owners over the past three centuries; the Dorrien family, the Foundling Hospital, Miss Wellesley and the Royal Forestry Society, that we can enjoy these wonderful woods today.

West of A416 approx one mile south-west of A41/A416 junction on edge of Berkhamsted. Footpaths and tracks throughout woods. Visit the Royal Forestry Society website for more information about access. **Grid: SP975062**

Abbey Pagoda

Near St Albans Abbey stands a magnificent Japanese Pagoda Tree. The tree is over 26m high and has a girth of 5.2m. Even though the tree is estimated to be over 250 years old, it is still a healthy specimen and has even flowered in recent years.

The tree is thought to have been planted in 1753 but this is anecdotal only as there is no hard evidence to verify its age. The oldest record of the tree is a photograph dated 1884 which shows Mr Hales the gardener and his wife, and C.S. and J.P. Nisbett sitting down beneath the tree.

Evidence suggests the species was introduced to Britain from France, where it had been introduced in 1747 from China. The Pagoda tree is native to China not Japan as its Latin name suggests.

James Gordon was a noted nurseryman of the 1700s who introduced and cultivated with success many exotic plants. He is credited with introducing the Pagoda tree to Britain in 1753, the same year the tree in Abbey grounds is thought to have been planted making it conceivable that the pagoda tree near the Abbey is one of the surviving James Gordon specimens.

This tree is in a private area of the grounds of St Albans Cathedral. **Grid: TL143070**

Domesday Oak

Set in beautiful wooded country south-west of Hitchin, Kings Walden is a scattered parish with the Kings Walden Park estate at its centre.

There are about 300 oaks across the estate, most of which are between 300 and 400 years old. The trees are believed to have been planted when the land (which was formerly arable) was planted as a deer park.

The oldest oak on the estate has been named the Domesday Oak because it is thought to be up to 1,000 years old. The tree has been pollarded and was probably part of a much older landscape, originally growing in a hedgerow.

This tree is on private land but can be seen from the footpath

Kings Walden Park (at Kings Walden) on a minor road three and a half miles north-east of Luton. The deer park lies east of hamlet and approached by public footpath to north of church. The tree can be seen from the footpath. **Grid: TL164231**

Croxley Green's Commemorative Trees

For more than a century Croxley Green has had a strong tradition of planting trees on the village green to commemorate royal and national events. Following an article by Councillor Janet Martin in the local Parish Council magazine, which mentioned nine special trees, project volunteers went along to further investigate and discovered three more.

Seven trees commemorate various important dates relating to the Royal family from Queen Victoria through to Queen Elizabeth II, including an oak planted to commemorate the Coronation of Edward VIII in 1936 – a coronation that never took place! The tree was planted just one day before Edward VIII's abdication.

Most of the 12 commemorative trees around The Green are oaks and bear plaques saying when and why they were planted. By the war memorial grows a tree in memory of those killed in the First World War, the Second World War and the Korean War. The Victory Oak, planted in November 1945, commemorates the end of the Second World War and a walnut commemorates the 50th anniversary of VE Day. A conifer commemorates the death of Sir Winston Churchill in 1965 and the most recent tree was planted to commemorate the Millennium and the gathering of 5,000 people to celebrate the event on The Green.

THIS OAK TREE COMMEMORATES THAT 5000 PEOPLE FROM CROXLEY GREEN GATHERED NEAR HERE ON 31 DECEMBER 1999 TO WELCOME IN THE NEW MILLENNIUM

Many of the tree-planting ceremonies have been recorded on camera. The photograph opposite depicts the planting of an oak in 1911 to commemorate the coronation of King George V which was attended by a large group of the local school children.

An oak at Providence Hall planted to celebrate the Coronation of Queen Elizabeth II

But the story does not end here because the Parish Council has agreed to plant (belatedly) a tree to commemorate the Golden Jubilee of Queen Elizabeth II thereby continuing the history of the royal family on The Green.

Local children attending a planting ceremony in 1911

Triangular plot of land on north edge of village. Turn north off A412 by church approx one mile east of Rickmansworth train station. **Grid: TQ070963**

Oxfordshire

FAIR MILE

JIMMY'S TREE

HUNTS GREEN CEDAR

THE MAHARAJAH'S WELL AND CHERRY ORCHARD

MEMORIAL AVENUE

SCOTS FARM OAKS

NETTLEBED WOODS

VICTORIA CROSS

'The first of this avenue was planted by H.R.H. Princess Margaret on 16th October 1953 to commemorate the coronation of Queen Elizabeth II, 2nd June 1953'

Fair Mile

In 1751 Sir Thomas Stapleton, then the Lord of the Manor of Benson, planted an elm tree avenue in the Fair Mile (the A4130 between Henley and Lower Assendon). It was much admired and quite a feature of the area but after 200 years the avenue had declined. It was decided to fell the elms and replace them with Turkey oaks. These were planted in 1953 to celebrate the coronation of Her Majesty Queen Elizabeth II.

The late Princess Margaret helped plant the first of these trees, cheered on by many Henley residents. The other trees were planted by George Butler, an apprentice at Waterers, the landscape gardeners at Twyford. 200 oak trees were planted at a cost of £2 2s each. More than 50 years later in 2007 191 remained with an average girth of 114 cm.

In 1978 another row of trees was planted to celebrate the Queen's Silver Jubilee. The Henley Mayor planted 180 lime trees between the road and the coronation oaks. By 2007 185 lime trees, with an average girth of 130 cm, formed the inner avenue.

The Fair Mile is the A4155 between Henley-on-Thames and the junction with the B480 at Lower Assendon. There are broad grass verges on both sides.
Grid: SU751838

Jimmy's Tree

This red oak grows by the grave stone to Jimmy, a Marmoset that died on 16th August 1937.

The local paper, the Henley Standard, reported that Miss Jeckyll, a local nursing sister in WWI, had two marmosets which she draped round her neck when shopping in Henley. Apparently, despite being cute and receiving much attention, they were inclined to bite those who came too close.

The stone bears the inscription:

'There isn't enough darkness in the world to quench the light of one small candle.'

Bernard Levin in Conducted Tour (1984) describes the quotation as an ancient proverb.

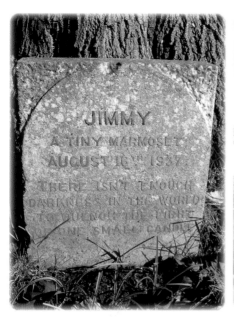

This tree was planted at the Henley-on-Thames end of the Fair Mile, close to the footpath sign to the Oxfordshire Way.

From Henley, take A4130 (Fair Mile) road towards Wallingford. This tree is on the north verge approx half a mile from Henley just past the signpost to the Oxfordshire Way footpath. **Grid: SU757833**

'There isn't enough darkness in the world to quench the light of one small candle'

Hunts Green Cedar

This young cedar was planted to commemorate the 1987 storm, in memory of the thousands of trees across the Chilterns that were blown down that night. It grows on the green at Hunts Green, Harpsden, near Henley-on-Thames.

This tree grows on the green at Hunts Green, Harpsden, to the south-west of Henley-on-Thames. **Grid: SU743805**

The Maharajah's Well and Cherry Orchard

The Maharajah's Well was officially opened on Queen Victoria's birthday in 1864. The path to the well was planted with an avenue of yew trees and four of the original trees survive today. The Cherry Orchard next to the well is often known by its Indian name, Ishree Bagh. The well and adjoining orchard were donated by the Maharajah of Benares to show his feelings for England and as a token of his friendship with Mr Reade. Edward Reade, of Ipsden, had carried out a similar gesture in 1831 by donating a well and mango grove to an Indian community.

101 cherry trees were planted in Stoke Row in order to provide an income to help with the up-keep of the well. A few still survive today.

The Maharajah's Well and Cherry Orchard are in the middle of Stoke Row village and designated as an open space. **Grid: SU678841**

Memorial Avenue

Volunteers have discovered many trees in the Chilterns planted in memory of local people. In Goring ten lime trees form an impressive avenue between the High Street and the church.

The avenue runs through Rectory Gardens which are dedicated to the memory of Peggy Edmondson, a young local woman who tragically drowned in the Thames in 1934 at the age of 21. Peggy had been born at the Rectory while her father was Rector. After the Rectory burned down about 1938, part of the land was given to the church as an extension to the graveyard and the remainder to the village as Peggy's memorial.

The avenue is in the centre of Goring village between the High Street and the church.
Grid: SU598807

Scots Farm Oaks

Two grand oak trees are found at Scots Farm. The smaller of the two is approaching 200 years old and is probably the offspring of its companion, a much older and larger oak.

30 years ago a tree house was constructed in this tree. Since then it has disintegrated, and the children who played in it grown up, but the oak lives on unaffected.

The larger tree has a massive girth of nearly 10m, indicating that it probably dates back nearly 400 years to the establishment of the farmhouse in the grounds of which it stands.

Despite its impressive girth this tree only stands about 10m tall as it has been pollarded many times throughout its life. This form of management may have supplied firewood for the farmhouse. The heartwood has rotted to create a huge hollow trunk.

'The tree house has disintegrated, and the children grown up, but the oak lives on unaffected'

Approx three quarters of a mile to the north-west of Checkendon, halfway between Dogmore End and Woodcote. Follow the narrow lane for approx half a mile.
Grid: SU662839

Nettlebed Woods

Nettlebed Woods are part of the local commons which are an ancient landscape with a long and varied history of land use. The commons form an intimate mosaic of habitats with ancient woodland, secondary woodland, ponds and boggy areas, and patches of lowland heath which are rare in this area. They are an important part of the area's biological diversity.

The commons have existed since the Middle Ages when they were demarcated by earth banks, some of which can still be seen today. The banks divided the commons into areas where commoners had different common rights – coppicing or pollarding trees to provide a steady supply of small timber; collecting fallen wood for fuel and fencing, and bracken for bedding; grazing animals; and extracting minerals such as sand, clay, gravel, chalk and flints. Clay pits and ancient earthworks are still visible in the woods which are criss-crossed by miles of track and paths.

The common at Nettlebed which surrounds Windmill Hill (the windmill burnt down in 1912) is wooded with a small piece of heathland, but it used to be a hive of industrial activity where bricks, tiles and pottery were all manufactured. 35,000 tiles were made for Wallingford Castle in 1365 and 200,000 bricks were made for the chapel tower at Stonor in 1416.

By the 19th century dozens of men were employed in Nettlebed extracting clay from the many pits close to the brick and tile works. The humps and hollows, many of which are now ponds, are all over Nettlebed Common. These, and one bottle kiln on the edge of the common, are all that remain today of this thriving industry. Once industry left, wildlife soon moved in and secondary woodland now covers much of the common closest to Nettlebed.

To the south is Lower Common Wood, an area of dense ancient woodland. The ancient earthwork known as Grim's Ditch runs through this part of the woods. Grim or Grimes is a Saxon word meaning 'fiend' and Grim's Ditch is believed to have been the northern boundary of a Celtic tribal territory and a line of defence. The sewage works in the middle of the wood was built by US Army Engineers during WWII who were billeted in a temporary camp of 2,000 soldiers, before their participation in the D-Day landings. Later the camp was taken over and used by European refugees, mostly Polish, some of whom still return to hunt for fungi in the autumn. The camp was demolished in the late 1940s, however a small monument to the US Engineers still stands by the roadside near Highmoor Trench.

Most of the common land round Nettlebed is part of the Nettlebed Estate. Joyce Grove and the surrounding lands were purchased by Robert Fleming of Fleming Merchant Bank in 1903. His grandsons, Peter the renowned travel writer who married Celia Johnson, star of the classic 1945 film *Brief Encounter*, and Ian, the celebrated spy novelist were both brought up there and Robert Fleming's great grandchildren now run the estate.

These woods lie in the triangle formed by A4130 and B481 roads, quarter of a mile south-east of Nettlebed. **Grid: SU710860**

Victoria Cross

The aerial photograph opposite shows 60 oaks planted in the shape of a cross on a hillside outside Henley. The trees are believed to have been planted to commemorate the Diamond Jubilee of Queen Victoria in 1897. Most of the original trees still survive and saplings were planted in 2009 to replace mature trees that had been lost.

Project volunteer Hilary noted that:

> *'The cross is hard to appreciate in full from the ground. A planting scheme is suggested by the straight lines but you would not know it was there unless you knew about it beforehand.'*

The Cross is a well known landmark in Henley and over the years it has generated much discussion. There are many theories as to why and when the cross was planted, including: to mark Queen Victoria's Golden or Diamond Jubilee; to celebrate associations with Malta (with a Maltese Cross); to mark the beginning of the Order of the Victoria Cross or the George Cross; or perhaps that the trees were planted by German PoWs in memory of the crew of a Luftwaffe bomber which crashed there.

Research by project volunteers has concluded that the most probable theory is that the 60 trees were planted in the shape of a Victoria Cross to commemorate Queen Victoria's Diamond Jubilee in 1897 when she celebrated 60 years on the throne.

The Oxfordshire Way runs through the cross but it is hard to appreciate from the ground

From Henley, take A4130 (Fair Mile) road towards Wallingford. After approx half a mile, follow the clearly signposted Oxfordshire Way footpath north, uphill for approx three quarters of a mile. **Grid: SU754843**

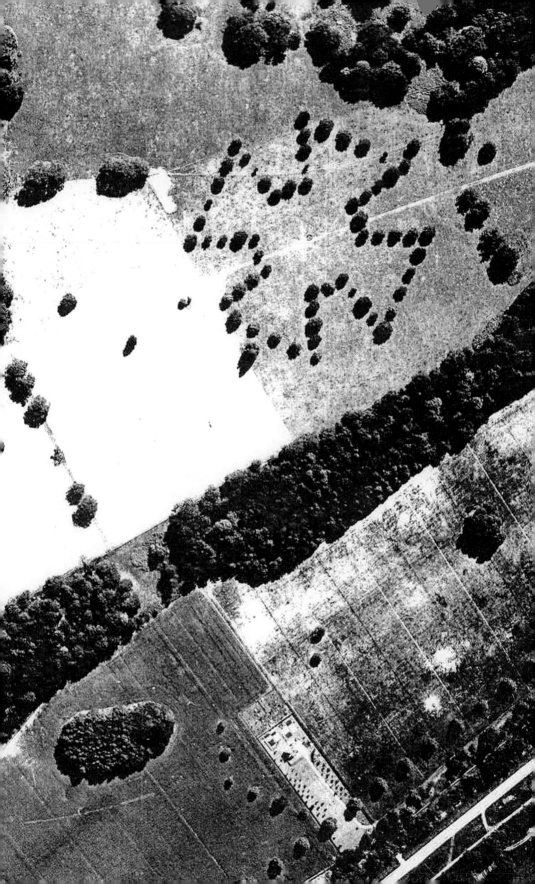

Appendices

THE WHY AND HOW OF TREE MEASUREMENT

HISTORY OF THE CHILTERN BODGERS

GLOSSARY OF TERMS AND USEFUL LINKS

TREES MENTIONED IN THE TEXT-SCIENTIFIC NAMES

CONTRIBUTORS

The Why and How of Tree Measurement

Perhaps, for the same reason as we climb mountains - because they are there! Trees which are large, old, commemorate an event or have a special connection with a locality deserve our particular attention, but it is worth measuring any tree, regardless of how ordinary it may seem today. By recording its size we may be augmenting existing information about a tree or creating a new record; in both cases future tree enthusiasts may value our work.

Man must have been measuring trees for hundreds of years. We know that coppice was cut when the stems were the correct size for the desired use, and timber trees were felled for particular uses, for example in ships or buildings. Much of this early measurement was probably done by experienced eyes without specific equipment. John Evelyn (1620-1706) measured trees and his *Sylva, or a Discourse of Forest Trees*, first published in 1664, is a classic early forestry book, written to encourage landowners to plant trees to supply the navy.

Edward Hoppus, Surveyor to the Corporation of the London Assurance, first drew up his timber-measuring tables in 1736, based on the quarter-girth measure. Timber measured in Hoppus feet was the standard method used to measure timber volume in this country until very recently. Foresters now mainly use metric measurements and a vast array of tables allow calculations of usable timber volume from measurements of standing individual trees and stands (where these comprise relatively uniformly-sized trees), as well as felled timber.

Interest in tree heights grew steadily throughout the 19th century, helped by the discovery in parts of the world, such as western North America, of conifers suitable for cultivation in Britain which were capable of reaching a great size and outstripping our native species.

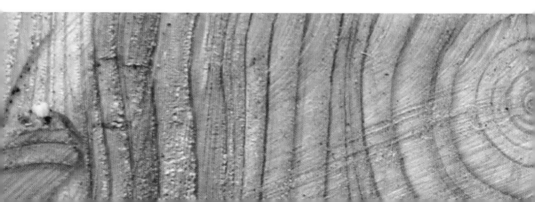

In modern times the late Alan Mitchell is best known for measuring thousands of trees throughout the British Isles. His *Field Guide to the Trees of Britain and Northern Europe*, first published by Collins in 1974, contains a huge wealth of information and references to tree sizes. The following information is taken largely from the excellent introduction to this book.

WHAT DO WE MEASURE?

Mitchell concentrates on two measurements to describe the size of a tree: the girth and the height. He defines a 'tree' for his book as 'a woody plant that commonly achieves a height of 6m on a single stem' and thus excludes shrubs, although he includes hazel: 'an abundant countryside species which might be thought to be a tree'.

The height and spread of a tree reach a maximum size then stop increasing and, after a variable time, will then start to decrease as senility sets in.

GIRTH

On the other hand the girth goes on increasing throughout a tree's life, and so can be used to estimate age. Although trees vary enormously, Mitchell found that most trees conform to a simple rule:

- mean growth in girth in most trees with a full crown is 2.5 cm a year; thus a tree in open ground with an 2.44m girth is about 100 years old
- a tree of similar size in a wood might be 200 years old
- growing in an avenue (or slightly hemmed in) it will be around 150 years old

Needless to say, Mitchell states some exceptions:

- most young trees grow much faster
- growth slows with age, so in very old trees the growth rate over the life of the tree will be less

Young oaks on a good site may grow 3.75-5 cm a year for their first 60-80 years, then at the standard rate until they attain a girth of 6-6.6m, then they slow further as a function of the loss of leafing crown.

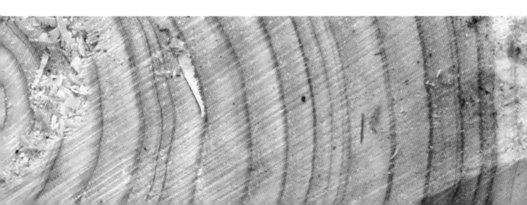

In certain species normal growth in girth is 5-7.5 cm per year. This includes: wellingtonia (may attain 15 cm per year), coast redwood, cedar of Lebanon, Monterey cypress, Sitka spruce, Douglas fir, western red cedar, western hemlock, cricket-bat willow, black Italian and other hybrid poplars, Turkey oak, tulip tree, London plane and most eucalyptus.

In the following normal growth soon falls below 2.5 cm per year; most small-growing trees, Scots pine, Norway spruce, horse chestnut and common lime.

Yew is a very special case. For the first 100 years a yew should attain 2.5 cm per year, but after that the rate of increase in girth slows, even when the crown retains full vigour and increases its spread annually. For this reason it is difficult to estimate the age of a yew from its girth, but as a rough guide: 2.44m = 100-150 years old, 4.88m = 300-400 years, 6.1m = 500-600 years and 9.5m = 850-1,000 years.

TREE RINGS

If the opportunity arises to inspect tree stumps, this should yield valuable information about the ages of the trees in a wood and their growth rates. Ideally the stumps should be freshly cut when the rings still show clearly. The structure of a tree stem is quite complex, but annual rings arise because in the spring large, thin-walled cells form close to the bark (these form the spring wood). Through the growing season new cells are progressively smaller and darker, with thicker walls. In the following season the new spring cells form next to the smallest and darkest cells from the previous year. This forms the annual ring. In some species such as birch and holly the rings may not be very clear.

Do bear in mind that the differentiation of cells to produce annual rings only happens in parts of the world when there is a break in the growing season caused by cold or drought.

Counting annual rings helps to reveal information about varying growth rates in different places due to site factors such as soil fertility and moisture availability. In a single tree there may also be marked variations in the width of the spring wood. These can be linked to variations in the weather; if the tree growth was slowed by drought or cold the spring wood will be narrower. Trees in a stand should put on a growth spurt after nearby trees have been felled (a thinning) and this will show in wider spring wood; this can useful when piecing together the management history of a wood. It is a reason why foresters want to thin out trees to encourage others to grow.

HEIGHT

Trees may be damaged in a variety of ways which shorten their height or they may be deliberately coppiced, pollarded or lopped. Nonetheless information about tree heights is valuable even if it is not a good predictor of age. The potential height of a species is of interest to gardeners, foresters and others, and the variation in heights attained by species on different sites is also of interest.

As Mitchell points out, some of the taller-growing species only introduced relatively recently have yet to show their full height potential in Britain. It was reported in February 2009 that Douglas fir has once again taken the lead in Britain's tallest tree race. The Stronardon Douglas Fir at Dunans Castle in Perthshire was measured at 63.79m, 12m taller than Nelson's Column.

WHAT TO RECORD

To be of most value tree measurements should use standard methods and provide a minimum of information as follows:

- the name and contact details of the person collecting the information
- date when the measurements were taken
- specific location of the tree: 8 figure Ordnance Survey Grid Reference; GPS co-ordinates (if available)
- species of the tree
- girth in metres measured 1.5m above the ground
- height in metres
- nearest village/town, with details of nearby features if this helps to locate the tree (this might be accompanied by a sketch map or photographs)
- setting, eg woodland, parkland, street, garden, farmland, churchyard
- directions to the tree
- name and contact details of the site owner and whether there is public access
- special name of the tree, if any
- any special or additional information about the tree

The Chilterns Special Trees and Woods Project produced a Special Tree Recording Form which can be downloaded from the website.

MEASURING TREE GIRTH

The girth is the circumference of the tree around its trunk. This is measured 1.5m above the highest point of the surrounding ground. You may find it useful to carry a stick of this length with you. Make a note if the adjacent ground appears disturbed in some way. Make sure that the tape is level all round the trunk. Check your first result once or twice and record the smallest figure. This should be in metres (to two decimal places).

MEASURING TREE HEIGHT

There are many ways of measuring tree height from the ground. Some use expensive devices such as an hypsometer or clinometer, or require the measurement of angles, with the use of trigonometry and accompanying tables or calculators.

Measuring tree height from the ground is relatively accurate when the surrounding ground is flat, when the proper top of the tree is visible, and when there is clear ground between the tree and the observer. Clearly in many situations some or none of these apply.

Try to apply the following rules:

- stand as far away from the tree as possible to see the top
- measure distance on the ground to the point below the highest part of the tree (this will often be to the centre of the trunk, but if the tree is leaning this may be away from the trunk)
- stand level with the tree, not above or below it on sloping ground
- check the height with a second measurement on a different baseline

If vision is obstructed, the true top is not visible or the baseline is impeded you may have to estimate the height and this should be recorded as such.

Trees with crown dieback should be measured to the highest live branch, with a separate measurement to the top of the original crown as this is also of interest.

History of the Chiltern Bodgers

The Chilterns are famous for the bodgers, the pole lathe turners, who used to work in the woods making parts for the nationally important furniture industry that developed here – so who were they?

Caroline Yeo wrote about the work of the bodgers in one of the project's newsletters:

The beech woods of the Chiltern Hills provided raw materials for the furniture industry and became famed for its chair production. The bodger made all turned parts of the chair, a craft which goes back over five hundred years. Today the popular meaning of bodge is to botch or mend clumsily. This derogatory term was applied to the 'old' traditional Chilterns woodland craftsmen by the 'new' men working in the furniture manufactories of Victorian High Wycombe.

The Chilterns bodgers, men like Ro Ridgeley at Penn Street, were in fact skilled craftsmen who made chair legs and braces. Selecting a mature (not too old), leggy (quickly grown) beech tree within a stand would have been just the first of the bodger's skills. Often working from a temporary woodland workshop near where he felled the trees, the bodger then used a selection of tools to create the turned parts of Windsor chairs. The tree would be sawn into billets the right length for the chair legs. The billet would be split into many pieces using a wedge. An axe would be used to shape the pieces into the shape of a chair leg and then the bodger would use a two handled draw knife to refine the shape of the leg. Finally, using a pole lathe (made of wood and string) the bodger would use chisels rested on the 'tool rest' to turn the wood to the required shape.

The finished chair legs would be left in the woods to season for a few weeks (depending on the weather) and then sold to local chair and furniture makers. Local craftsmen like Jack Goodchild of Naphill bought from bodgers. Jack Goodchild was the last independent chair maker in the Chilterns and examples of his work can be found in the Wycombe Museum.

Stuart King also wrote about the old chair bodgers of Buckinghamshire who are now relegated to history, the last few of them doggedly clinging on to their traditional way of life until the late 1950s:

They are all gone now but their legacy is everywhere. You are supported by their craftsmanship every time you sit in an old Windsor chair. Every leg, spindle and stretcher contains the spirit of these men. The essence of the beech woods is still there. Much has been written of these pole lathe turners and the contribution they made to the furniture manufacturing town of High Wycombe and, as is the way with history, distortion and myth tend to creep into the story. I have seen references to chair bodgers as being 'itinerant' - they never were. They were family men with a cottage to go home to every night. For the chair bodgers of Speen, Lacey Green and Great Hampden villages the buying of timber was a great annual social event. The Duke of Buckingham's Hampden estate owned much of the local beech woods and sold 'stands' or parcels of standing timber every autumn. A catalogue was issued to all prospective purchasers detailing the number of trees and species in each lot, its location and accessibility. Armed with a catalogue the local bodgers spent some time visiting each location and weighing up the pros and cons of each lot. Were there enough trees to keep them busy for the next twelve months? Was it easy to get a wagon on to the area? How far from home (walking distance) was it? What happened if your favourite lot proved too popular and you lost the bidding? It was all these considerations and uncertainties that made the auction such a big day in the chair bodgers' calendar.

Bodgers by
Osvalda Teiser

The Project also recorded a number of oral histories to capture other stories of the people of the Chilterns. Mr Richard Hearne was interviewed by Rosalie Bullock:

William Hearne established a successful furniture-making business in 1840 which was later called Dancer and Hearne. Over the years, the business has evolved with changing timber markets and availability, technology and demand. In 1938, 450,000 chairs were made by Dancer and Hearne, mainly in the Penn Street factory, while the Lindsay Avenue factory in High Wycombe concentrated on cabinets and dining tables. Mr Hearne's memories and entries from diaries compiled by his grandfather and father give a wonderful insight into the furniture trade. For example, in 1935 a diary entry of 20th December states: 'Roads still bad. Horses can't get in with timber', illustrating that access in and out of woodlands has always been a problem, not just for the modern forester with his large harvesting machines.

Glossary of Terms and Useful Links

Acres – traditional measure of area (based on a furlong = 220 yards by a chain = 22 yards) 1 acre = approximately 0.4 hectares.

Ancient Tree Hunt - a search to record old and veteran trees, see *www.ancient-tree-hunt.org.uk*

Bodgers – the traditional pole lathe turners of the Chilterns, who turned chair parts such as legs etc until the mid 20th century.

Chilterns Conservation Board – set up to care for the Chilterns AONB, see *www.chilternsaonb.org*

Chiltern Society – owns Bottom Wood, see *www.chilternsociety.org.uk*

Coppicing – the regular cutting of areas of broadleaved trees to utilise the poles and encourage new poles to grow from the cut stumps.

Domesday Book – a major survey carried out after the Norman Conquest in 1086 to record land ownership for taxation and political purposes.

Felled – an area of trees that have been cut down.

Forestry Commission – the government department that regulates forestry and also manages the nation's forest estate. See *www.forestry.gov.uk* which includes information on trees and forestry, grants and regulations.

Hectares (ha) – metric measure of area 100 metres x 100 metres = 10,000 square metres, one hectare = 2.47 acres

Inventory of Ancient Woodlands – a map showing woods known to have existed since 1600 AD; used by Natural England and the Forestry Commission.

Lopped – branches that have been cut off a trunk.

Metre - 1 metre = 3.28 feet

National Trust – a charity which owns many sites in the Chilterns including the Ashridge and Bradenham estates, see *www.nationaltrust.org. uk*

Pollards – trees that have been cut back above the height of browsing animals such as cattle and deer, so that new shoots can grow without being eaten. Normally found in parks, wood pasture on commons and in hedgerows.

Royal Forestry Society – a national charity for those interested in trees and forestry. The Royal Forestry Society is based in Tring with a specialist forestry library and owns Hockeridge and Pancake woods in the Chilterns. The Society has a comprehensive website, see *www.rfs.org. uk*

Scheduled Ancient Monument – a designated archaeological or historic site, eg Iron Age hillforts in the Chilterns – many are now found in woodland, see *www.english-heritage.org.uk*

Site of Special Scientific Interest (SSSI) – a designation to protect important land for nature conservation, see *www.naturalengland.org.uk*

Small Woods Association – a national charity for woodland owners and others interested in the management of small woods, see *www.smallwoods.org.uk*

The Tree Register of the British Isles – a national charity which records champion trees, see *www.tree-register.org*

Woodland Trust – a woodland owning charity. Owns a number of important woods in the Chilterns including Tring Park, Penn Wood and Harpsden Wood, see *www.woodlandtrust.org.uk*

Veteran trees - trees that have started to decline and show wounds from storms, tree surgery work etc. These rot holes and breaks are valuable habitat for a wide range of organisms from rare beetles to bats.

Trees Mentioned in the Text - Scientific Names

INTRODUCED TREES

English Name	Scientific name
Black walnut	Juglans nigra
Tulip tree	Liriodendron tulipifera
London plane	Platanus x hispanica
Turkey oak	Quercus cerris
Red oak	Quercus rubra
Japanese pagoda tree	Sophora japonica

CONIFERS

English Name	Scientific name
Cedar of Lebanon	Cedrus libani
Norway spruce	Picea abies
Scots pine	Pinus sylvestris
Wellingtonia	Sequoiadendron giganteum

NATIVE TREES

English Name	Scientific name
Field maple	Acer campestre
Sycamore	Acer pseudoplatanus
Silver birch	Betula pendula
Sweet chestnut	Castanea sativa
Hornbeam	Carpinus betulus
Hawthorn	Crataegus monogyna
Beech	Fagus sylvatica
Ash	Fraxinus excelsior
Holly	Ilex aquifolium
Wild cherry	Prunus avium
English (or Pedunculate) oak	Quercus robur
Rowan or Mountain ash	Sorbus aucuparia
Whitebeam	Sorbus aria
Wild service tree	Sorbus torminalis
Wild pear	Pyrus pyraster
Small leaved lime	Tilia cordata
Yew	Taxus baccata

Contributors

Our thanks to all of the volunteers who took part in the Special Trees and Woods Project. A number of the stories in this book were a team effort and our apologies to anyone who helped but has been missed from the list below or for images that have been wrongly attributed; it is unintentional.

The Special Trees and Woods Project volunteers discovered several hundred stories about trees and woods in the Chilterns. These are just a few of our favourites – there are more on the website *www.chilternsaonb. org/special.*

Thanks are also owed to Liz Manley and Rachel Sanderson who, between them, coordinated the volunteer team.

ACKNOWLEDGEMENTS
Photography by John Morris

FOREWORD
Written by Thomas Pakenham
Artwork by Margaret Taperell

INTRODUCTION

Written by John Morris
Photography by June Kingsbury and David Burton
Artwork by Rachel Wallace and Maria Turner

SHARPENHOE CLAPPERS

Story by Rachel Sanderson
Photography by John Morris

WITCHES BEECH

Story by Rachel Marshall
Photography by John Morris

WHIPSNADE TREE CATHEDRAL

Story and photography by Barry Gowers

MURDEROUS MARKER

Story by and photography by Rachel Sanderson

CLAYFIELD COPSE

Story and photography by Hilary Beck-Burridge

GEORGE'S CEDAR

Story and photography by Bruce Brown

BURNHAM BEECHES

Story by Liz Manley
Photography by John Morris, Chris Read and
Odette Carden-Fleet
Artwork by Laraine Healey

BLASTED OAK

Story by Anne Butterworth
Photography by John Morris

BULSTRODE CAMP

Story and photography by Russell and Chris Read

IBSTONE YEW

Story and photography by Hilary Beck-Burridge

LOW SCRUBS

Story and photography by John Morris

TURVILLE PARK LIME AVENUE

Story by Hilary Beck-Burridge

Photography by Martin and Hilary Beck-Burridge

ELEPHANT TREE

Story by Russell and Chris Read

Photography by John Morris and Russell Read

GIANT CHERRY

Story by Russell and Chris Read

Photography by Ivor Weston

MUSHROOM TREE

Story by Liz Manley

Photography by Martin Beck-Burridge

NAPHILL COMMON

Story by Trevor Hussey

Photography by John Morris and Phillip Hussey

Artwork by Susan Wharton

UMBRELLA TREE

Story by Trevor and Philip Hussey

Photography by Philip Hussey

Artwork by Trevor Hussey

THE SHOE TREE

Story by Russell and Chris Read

Photography by Steve Colgan

PALACE PLANE

Story by Janet Pullen

Photography by Martin Beck-Burridge

PARSONAGE WOOD

Story and photography by Russell and Chris Read

PRIESTFIELD ARBORETUM
Story by Barbara Rippington
Photography by Graham Bradshaw, Rachael Marshall,
Russell Read and David Watson

CRUCIFIX TREE
Story and photography by John Morris

TYLERS GREEN MEMORIAL TREES
Story by Russell and Chris Read
Photography by John Morris and Russell Read

CLIVENDEN
Story and photography by Janet Pullen

TAPLOW TULIP
Story and photography by Graham Bradshaw

THE 'GREATEST ASH'
Story and photography by Graham Bradshaw

REMNANTZ WALNUT
Story and photography by Janet Pullen

SPARKY'S ASH
Story by Liz Manley
Photography by Claire Forrest and John Morris

PULLINGSHILL WOOD
Story by June Kingsbury
Photography by John Morris and June Kingsbury
Artwork by Keith Beckett-Hester

PULPIT HILL
Story by Vicki Billings
Photography by John Morris
Artwork by Judy Nash

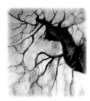

PENN WOOD
Story by Rachel Sanderson
Photography by Graham Bradshaw
Artwork by Patricia Lynch and Isabel Fallow

HODGEMOOR WOOD
Story by Paula Lacey
Photography by Joanna Hall

QUEEN ELIZABETH OAK
Story by Russell and Chris Read
Photography by Russell Read

FAWLEY COURT
Story by Hilary Beck-Burridge
Photography by Martin and Hilary Beck-Burridge

BOTTOM WOOD
Story and photography by John Morris

WOODS OF THE WHIPPENDELL VALLEY
Story by Brian Thomson
Photography by Brian and Katy Thomson

ASHRIDGE
Story by Liz Hamilton
Photography by John Morris and Graham Bradshaw
Artwork by Jackie Carden

WAR WOUNDS
Story by Bob Davis
Photography by Paul Jerem

HOCKRIDGE AND PANCAKE WOODS
Story by Andrew Muir
Photography by John Morris

ABBEY PAGODA
Story and photography by Brian Lee

DOMESDAY OAK
Story by Verity Roberts
Photography by Chris Barclay

CROXLEY GREEN'S COMMEMORATIVE TREES
Story by Fred and Joyce Bush
Photography by Brian Thomson and Joyce Bush

FAIR MILE
Story and photography by Hilary Beck-Burridge

JIMMY'S TREE
Story by Janet Pullen
Photography by Janet Pullen and Martin Beck-Burridge

HUNTS GREEN CEDAR
Story by Tony Austin
Photography by Martin Beck-Burridge

THE MAHARAJAH'S WELL AND CHERRY ORCHARD
Story by Liz Manley
Photography by John Morris

MEMORIAL AVENUE
Story and photography by Rachel Sanderson

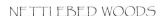

SCOTS FARM OAKS
Story by Doug Powell
Photography by Charlotte Snowden and David Watson

NETTLEBED WOODS
Story by Hilary Beck-Burridge
Photography by John Morris and Graham Bradshaw

VICTORIA CROSS
Story by Jane Osborn, Tony Austin and Hilary Beck-Burridge
Photography by Hilary Beck-Burridge
Black and white aerial photo from Henley Standard

THE HOW AND WHY OF TREE MEASUREMENT
Text by Liz Hamilton
Photography by John Morris

HISTORY OF THE CHILTERN BODGERS
Text by Caroline Yeo, Stuart King and Rosalie Bullock
Artwork by Osvalda Teiser

GLOSSARY OF TERMS AND LIST OF TREE NAMES
Compiled by John Morris and Rachel Sanderson
Photography by John Morris

Thanks also go to Jerry Page, National Trust Warden of Pulpit Hill Wood; Julia Wise of the Bucks Historical Record Department; and Brett Thorn, Keeper of Archaeology, Buckinghamshire County Museum.

Images used for each county page:

BEDFORDSHIRE - Sharpenhoe Clappers by John Morris

BERKSHIRE - Clayfield Copse by Hilary Beck-Burridge

BUCKINGHAMSHIRE - Pulpit Hill by John Morris

HERTFORDSHIRE - Golden Valley at Ashridge by John Morris

OXFORDSHIRE - Victoria Cross by Hilary Beck-Burridge

APPENDICES - Pigotts Wood by John Morris